The Macat Library
世界思想宝库钥匙丛书

解析理查德·H.泰勒 / 卡斯·R.桑斯坦

《助推：如何做出有关健康、财富和幸福的更优决策》

AN ANALYSIS OF

RICHARD H. THALER & CASS R. SUNSTEIN'S

NUDGE

Improving Decisions about Health,
Wealth and Happiness

Mark Egan ◎ 著

江丹 ◎ 译

上海外语教育出版社
外教社 SHANGHAI FOREIGN LANGUAGE EDUCATION PRESS

MACAT

目　录

引 言 ⋯⋯⋯⋯⋯⋯⋯⋯⋯⋯⋯⋯⋯⋯⋯⋯⋯⋯⋯ 1

　理查德·H.泰勒和卡斯·R.桑斯坦简介　2

　《助推》的主要内容　3

　《助推》的学术价值　5

第一部分：学术渊源 ⋯⋯⋯⋯⋯⋯⋯⋯⋯⋯⋯ 7

　1. 作者生平与历史背景　8

　2. 学术背景　12

　3. 主导命题　16

　4. 作者贡献　20

第二部分：学术思想 ⋯⋯⋯⋯⋯⋯⋯⋯⋯⋯⋯ 25

　5. 思想主脉　26

　6. 思想支脉　30

　7. 历史成就　35

　8. 著作地位　39

第三部分：学术影响 ⋯⋯⋯⋯⋯⋯⋯⋯⋯⋯⋯ 43

　9. 最初反响　44

　10. 后续争议　48

　11. 当代印迹　52

　12. 未来展望　56

术语表 ⋯⋯⋯⋯⋯⋯⋯⋯⋯⋯⋯⋯⋯⋯⋯⋯⋯⋯ 60

人名表 ⋯⋯⋯⋯⋯⋯⋯⋯⋯⋯⋯⋯⋯⋯⋯⋯⋯⋯ 64

CONTENTS

WAYS IN TO THE TEXT 69

Who Are Richard H. Thaler and Cass R. Sunstein? 70

What Does *Nudge* Say? 71

Why Does *Nudge* Matter? 73

SECTION 1: INFLUENCES 77

Module 1: The Authors and the Historical Context 78

Module 2: Academic Context 83

Module 3: The Problem 88

Module 4: The Authors' Contribution 93

SECTION 2: IDEAS 99

Module 5: Main Ideas 100

Module 6: Secondary Ideas 105

Module 7: Achievement 111

Module 8: Place in the Authors' Work 116

SECTION 3: IMPACT 121

Module 9: The First Responses 122

Module 10: The Evolving Debate 127

Module 11: Impact and Influence Today 132

Module 12: Where Next? 137

Glossary of Terms 142

People Mentioned in the Text 146

Works Cited 149

引 言

要 点

- 经济学家理查德·H.泰勒和法学家卡斯·R.桑斯坦是美国杰出的学者，他们曾于20世纪90年代和21世纪初在芝加哥大学共事。

- 在《助推：如何做出有关健康、财富和幸福的更优决策》一书中，泰勒和桑斯坦提出了"自由主义的温和专制主义"*、"选择架构"*和"助推"*等思想，建议政府利用这些决策工具帮助民众做出更加有利于健康、财富和幸福的决策，但是同时不干涉他们的选择自由。

- 《助推》影响了英、美等国的政策制定。该书是近年来最具影响力的公共政策图书之一。

理查德·H.泰勒和卡斯·R.桑斯坦简介

《助推：如何做出有关健康、财富和幸福的更优决策》的作者之一理查德·H.泰勒生于1945年，1974年在美国罗切斯特大学获得经济学博士学位，1995年起在美国芝加哥大学任教。他在职业生涯的早期接触到了以色列心理学家丹尼尔·卡尼曼*和阿莫斯·特沃斯基*的学术思想。二者对他有很大的影响。他后来成为芝加哥布斯商学院的行为科学*和经济学教授。泰勒的杰出贡献使他成为行为经济学*（经济学的一个分支学科，利用心理学的研究结果来制定经济决策模型）的奠基人。许多学者预测泰勒可能成为未来的诺贝尔奖得主[1]。（理查德·H.泰勒于2017年获得诺贝尔经济学奖——译者加。）

卡斯·R.桑斯坦出生于1954年，1978年毕业于哈佛大学法学院。他于 1981 年至 2008 年在美国芝加哥大学任教，在此期间研究行为经济学在法学领域的应用。他总共发表了 500 多篇不同主题的文章。2009 年至 2012 年间，他在奥巴马政府 * 任职。桑斯坦现为美国哈佛大学罗伯特·沃姆斯利校级教授（哈佛大学校级教授的称号始设于 1935 年，旨在表彰那些做出开创性工作，跨越学科界限的学者。校级教授可以在哈佛大学的任何一个学院进行研究——译者加）。他是当今世界上被引用最多的、最具影响力的法学家之一。

20 世纪 90 年代，泰勒和桑斯坦开始在芝加哥大学撰写《助推》一书。学术界认为芝加哥大学是芝加哥学派 * 的发源地。芝加哥学派支持新古典主义经济学 * 的经济理论。根据新古典主义经济学，人们在完全信息的基础上做出理性的经济决策。尽管《助推》的大部分内容强烈反对这种假设，实际上泰勒和桑斯坦并不排斥芝加哥学派的所有观点，他们的研究恰恰基于芝加哥学派经济学家米尔顿·弗里德曼 * 的思想即人们应该有"选择的自由"。[2]

《助推》的主要内容

在《助推》一书中，泰勒和桑斯坦认为政府可以在尊重民众自由选择权的同时引导他们做出更优决策。

政府可以通过设计更有效的"选择架构"来实现这一切。选择设计者设计决策环境，由人们自己做出选择。书中举了一个简单的例子：一名学校自助餐厅经理通过改变食品的摆放方式促进健康饮食。她将蔬菜摆放在最前面，以此增加孩子们对健康食品的消费量。像这种通过改变选择架构以鼓励某种行为的模式被泰勒和桑斯坦称为"助推"。驾驶员使用的卫星导航系统，鼓励人们走楼梯不坐电梯的标志，政府发布的营养指南等都是助推的实例。这些助推鼓励人们采取某一行为，但是并不强迫人们一定要这么做。

泰勒和桑斯坦认为政府应该助推民众做出更优决策。然而，必须由民众自己判断这些决策是否更优，而不是由政府替他们做出判断。泰勒和桑斯坦把这种思想称为"自由主义的温和专制主义"。

自由主义和温和专制主义*听起来相互矛盾对立。自由主义强调个人自由，反对政府干预。温和专制主义者则认为自己是他人利益的代言人。但是泰勒和桑斯坦通过"选择架构"的概念调和了这对矛盾。他们认为在不限制选择自由的条件下，干预是可以被允许的。他们列举了一个公司鼓励其员工为退休生活而储蓄的例子。[3]该公司采用的助推手段是将员工纳入养老金计划，但如果员工不想加入的话，他们可以选择退出。一般情况下员工不太会去修改默认选项，储蓄率因此而增长。同时，这种选择设计也保护了员工可以不加入养老金计划的自由。

泰勒和桑斯坦认为，助推可以带来有意义的、可预见的影响，从而否认了主流经济学派对人类行为的基本假设。主流经济学派的研究建立在"理性人"*这一假设基础之上。"理性人"具有完备的知识、无限的认知能力和完美的自我控制能力。助推手段无法影响这些"理性人"。《助推》一书则认为在真实的社会中，普通人在知识完备程度、认知能力和自我控制能力方面具有天然的局限性。认知偏差*（导致人们偏离理性判断和行为的认知方式）和社会压力影响着他们的决策。助推能够影响这些普通人。

泰勒和桑斯坦将经济模型中的理想决策者称为"经济人"*，将现实世界中的普通决策者称为"社会人"*。他们认为助推能够帮助社会人做出更加明智的决策。为了支持其论点，他们引用了数十年来的心理学和行为经济学的研究成果来证明心理因素会导致人们做出糟糕的决策。

泰勒和桑斯坦认为他们提出的思考模式是美国政治"真正的第三条道路"*。[4] 他们希望助推思想不但能够吸引有支持政府干预传统的民主党*，还能够吸引有反对政府干预传统的共和党*。

《助推》的学术价值

《助推》是近年来出版的最具影响力的公共政策著作之一。助推思想在公共政策、学术研究和私营企业等领域都产生了深远的影响。

《助推》问世后，英国右翼保守党*几乎立即接受了助推思想。2010年，英国首相戴维·卡梅伦*创建了全球第一个政府"助推小组"*，其官方名称为"行为洞察团队"。该团队的成功使得美国政府于2015年设立了"社会与行为科学团队"*。德国、荷兰、芬兰、新加坡和澳大利亚等国政府也深受助推思想的影响。[5]

《助推》引起了学术界的极大兴趣，它已在经济学、心理学、公共卫生、市场营销、社会学、医学、政治学、犯罪学、哲学等多个学科领域被引用5 000多次。[6] 上述众多领域运用助推思想分析新语境、解决新问题。

《助推》思想在商界也得到了实践。2008年《哈佛商业评论》登载了一篇文章，描述企业如何运用助推手段向客户推销产品。[7]《福布斯》2014年的一篇文章描述了行为经济学对整个广告业的影响。[8] 谷歌也将助推思想应用到了员工自助餐厅中。[9]

泰勒和桑斯坦自其著作问世起就一直致力于推广助推思想。泰勒向英国政府助推小组提出了有关税收和能源效率方面的政策建议。[10] 桑斯坦在2009年至2012年担任白宫信息与法规事务办公室主任期间也运用了助推思想。两位作者在访谈、论文和其他著作中都回应了对《助推》的批评。

对于任何对行为科学感兴趣的人来说，《助推》都是必读之书。

---

1. 诺亚·史密斯："五位应该获得诺贝尔奖的经济学家"，《彭博视野》，2014 年 12 月 9 日，登录日期 2015 年 9 月 4 日，http://www.bloombergview.com/articles/2014-12-09/ five-economists-who-deserve-nobels。

2. 理查德·H.泰勒和卡斯·R.桑斯坦：《助推：如何做出有关健康、财富和幸福的更优决策》，纽约：耶鲁大学出版社，2008 年，第 5 页。

3. 泰勒和桑斯坦：《助推》，第 109 页。

4. 泰勒和桑斯坦：《助推》，第 252 页。

5. 行为洞察团队："行为洞察团队 2013—2015 年更新报告"，登录日期 2015 年 9 月 4 日，http://www.behaviouralinsights.co.uk/wp-content/uploads/2015/07/BIT_Update-Report-Final-2013-2015.pdf。

6. 截至 2015 年 9 月 26 日谷歌学术记录了 5 495 条引用《助推》的文本，登录日期 2015 年 9 月 26 日，https://scholar.google.com/scholar?cites=16854468477297806637&as_sdt=2005&sciodt=0,5&hl=en。

7. 丹尼尔·G.戈德斯坦等："把你的客户推向更好的选择"，《哈佛商业评论》，2008 年 12 月，登录日期 2015 年 9 月 4 日，https//hbr.org/2008/12/nudge-your-customers-toward-better-choices。

8. 约翰·奥维德："行为经济学让广告业朝着正确的方向前进"，《福布斯》，2014 年 2 月 5 日，登录日期 2015 年 9 月 26 日，http://www.forbes.com/sites/johnowrid/ 2014/ 02/05/behavioural-economics-gives-the-advertising-industry-a-nudge-in-the-right-direction/。

9. 克里夫·广："自助餐厅，谷歌健康成长"，《快公司杂志》，2012 年 3 月 19 日，登录日期 2015 年 9 月 4 日，http://www. fastcompany.com/1822516/cafeteria-google-gets-healthy。

10. 道格拉斯·克莱门特："理查德·H.泰勒访谈录"，《地区杂志》，2013 年 10 月 3 日，登录日期 2015 年 9 月 4 日，https://www. minneapolisfed.org/publications/the-region/interview-with-richard-thaler。

第一部分：学术渊源

1 作者生平与历史背景

要点 🔑

- 《助推》是近年来出版的关于公共政策的最具影响力的图书之一。
- 《助推》的作者受到心理学关于人类决策研究的影响，尤其是来自以色列心理学家丹尼尔·卡尼曼和阿莫斯·特沃斯基的影响。
- 《助推》的作者采用行为经济学的理论提出政府应当在尊重民众自由选择权的同时，采用助推的方式帮助他们做出更优决策。

为何要读这部著作？

2008 年，芝加哥大学行为科学和经济学教授理查德·H. 泰勒和时任芝加哥大学法学教授的卡斯·R. 桑斯坦合著的力作《助推：如何做出有关健康、财富和幸福的更优决策》面世。

《助推》的主要观点是政府可以在不干涉民众选择自由的同时帮助他们做出更优决策。这个目标可以通过设计决策环境来实现。泰勒和桑斯坦将这个决策环境称之为"选择架构"。例如，为促进健康饮食，自助餐厅将水果摆放在取餐台的最前面而将甜点摆放在最后；公司将其员工默认纳入退休金计划，不愿意加入该计划的员工也可以选择退出；网站根据用户的购买记录推荐产品。上述案例中，在某些特定行为受到鼓励的同时，既没有禁止其他选项，也没有强迫人们做出决策。泰勒和桑斯坦将此类干预行为称为"助推"。

《助推》在其出版后的七年中，共被引用 5 000 多次，对一系列学科产生了影响。[1] 该书直接影响了英国和美国政府最高层的决策。它还影响了营销、咨询、管理等众多行业。《助推》一直是研究决策和行为改变的必读之书。

> "是的，常识确实存在……这就是读者对泰勒和桑斯坦的'助推'思想的反应。该书引人入胜、见解深刻。它证明了大多数人做决策时，并非像基础经济学教科书中描述的那样理性。它还为个人和社会提出了丰富的建议，人们可以据此做出更理智的决策。"
>
> —— 本杰明·M. 弗里德曼："引导力"，《纽约时报》

作者生平

理查德·H. 泰勒于 1974 年获得经济学博士学位。尽管泰勒接受传统经济学的教育，学习以完全理性"经济人"假说为前提的决策模型，但他在职业生涯早期，受到以色列心理学家丹尼尔·卡尼曼和阿莫斯·特沃斯基的影响，他们的见解对人类理性的假设构成了最有力的冲击。泰勒后来将他们的思想（以及心理学的其他研究）融入经济学，开拓了行为经济学新领域，成为该领域的创始人。《助推》是基于行为经济学理论的著作。

卡斯·R. 桑斯坦 1975 年毕业于哈佛大学法学院，获得法学博士学位。他在整个职业生涯中著述颇丰，其中将行为经济学应用到法学领域的文章产生了极大的影响力。桑斯坦也是著名的司法极简主义*支持者。司法极简主义是一种法律哲学，主张针对宪法性法律*（属于宪法范畴的一系列法律）进行细微的、个案的具体解释。这种思想可能反映了桑斯坦对《助推》中所讨论的渐进式的、"温和"的干预的偏好。

20 世纪 90 年代至 21 世纪初，泰勒与桑斯坦在芝加哥大学共事，在此期间他们合作写下了《助推》一书。具有讽刺意味的是，芝加哥学派被认为是传统新古典主义经济学的发源地，而《助推》则是对传统经济学的反叛，它驳斥了传统经济学的基本假设之一，即人们以完全理性的方式做出经济决策。然而，《助推》并不完全否定芝加哥学派的思想，"助推"的概念恰恰以芝加哥学派经济学家米尔顿·弗里德曼的观点为基础，即人们有权"自由选择"。[2]

创作背景

在《助推》的开头几章中，泰勒和桑斯坦介绍了助推思想的历史背景：关于人类决策问题有两个对立的学术流派。

一个流派采用新古典主义经济学的理性决策模型。自 1946 年第二次世界大战*结束以来，理性决策模型一直是主流经济学思想的基石。它提出了一种抽象的人类行为模型，在这个模型中，人的行为完全理性。

另一个流派遵循行为经济学思想。这些思想由理性决策模型发展而来。行为经济学认为理性决策模型不切实际。行为经济学基于心理学对人在现实生活中的行为的研究，目标是建立更真实的人类决策模型。丹尼尔·卡尼曼和阿莫斯·特沃斯基关于人类决策缺陷的研究对行为经济学影响深远。

《助推》出版于 2008 年全球金融危机*期间。在此期间以及随后的几年内，新古典主义经济学因未能预见到此次金融危机而受到媒体人士[3]和学者[4]的批评。2010 年，芝加哥学派经济学家理查德·波斯纳*承认，2008 年金融危机已经给"整个经济学界带来了挑战，特别是对芝加哥学派的挑战"。[5]这场金融危机发生后，作为理解经济行为的另一种思路，人们对行为经济学的兴趣与日俱增。[6]

2010 年，后来成为英国首相的戴维·卡梅伦指出了金融危机的另一个后果，他说："在英国政治或美国政治中，我们需要记住一个最重要的事实：我们已经没钱了。"[7] 在同一次演讲中，卡梅伦引用并赞同行为经济学的观点，认为其可以帮助"建设一个更强大的社会但不必花费大笔开支"。[8] 上述两个原因都为《助推》所描述的行为经济学思想创造了一种更容易被接受的氛围，在英国尤其如此。

1. 截至 2015 年 9 月 26 日谷歌学术记录了 5 495 条引用《助推》的文本，登录日期 2015 年 9 月 26 日，https://scholar.google.com/scholar?cites=16854468477297806637&as_sdt=2005&sciodt=0,5&hl=en。
2. 理查德·H. 泰勒和卡斯·R. 桑斯坦：《助推：如何做出有关健康、财富和幸福的更优决策》，纽约：耶鲁大学出版社，2008 年，第 5 页。
3. FT 观点："经济学需要反映危机后的世界"，《金融时报》，2014 年 9 月 25 日，登录日期 2015 年 10 月 15 日，http://www.ft.com/cms/s/0/f9f65e88–44a3–11e4–ab0c–00144feabdc0.html#axzz3ojq0z1zz。
4. 保罗·克鲁格曼："经济学家们是如何犯下如此大错的？"，《纽约时报》，2009 年 9 月 6 日，登录日期 2015 年 9 月 26 日，http://www.econ.ucdavis.edu/faculty/kdsalyer/LECTURES/Ecn200e/krugman_macro.pdf。
5. 约翰·卡西迪："轰炸之后"，《纽约客》，2010 年 1 月 11 日，登录日期 2015 年 9 月 26 日，http://www.newyorker.com/magazine/2010/01/11/after-the-blowup。
6. 加里·贝克尔："行为金融来拯救？"，《经济学人》，2009 年 8 月 18 日，登录日期 2015 年 9 月 26 日，http://www.economist.com/blogs/freeexchange/2009/08/behavioural_fiance_to_the_res。
7. 戴维·卡梅伦："谈下一代的政府"，TED，2010 年 2 月，登录日期 2015 年 9 月 4 日，http://www.ted.com/talks/david_cameron?language=en。
8. 卡梅伦："谈下一代的政府"。

2 学术背景

要点 🔑

- 在新古典主义经济学提出的人类决策模型中人具备完全的理性。
- 泰勒吸收了心理学家卡尼曼和特沃斯基的思想，认为人们有时会以可预测的方式持续做出"非理性"行为。
- 泰勒将对"非理性"行为的研究融入传统经济学，成为行为经济学的奠基人。

著作语境

理查德·H.泰勒和卡斯·R.桑斯坦的《助推：如何做出有关健康、财富和幸福的更优决策》以行为经济学理论为基础。行为经济学将心理学的研究融入经济学，旨在建立更为真实的人类决策模型。美国行为经济学家科林·凯莫勒*和乔治·罗文斯坦*在对行为经济学史的回顾中，认为亚当·斯密*1759年出版的伦理学著作《道德情操论》*对个体行为的心理学原理见解深刻，因而将其视作该学科的基础理论。[1]

凯莫勒和罗文斯坦认为现代行为经济学始于20世纪下半叶，源于对新古典主义经济学中理性选择理论*的批判。理性选择理论描述了一种简化的人类决策模型，在该模型中人被视为"理性人"，他们拥有完全的信息、完美的认知能力和无限的自我控制能力。泰勒和桑斯坦在《助推》中批评这些假设不切实际。那些理性人被描绘得"能够像阿尔伯特·爱因斯坦一样思维缜密，有与IBM的'蓝色巨人'（超级计算机）一样强大的记忆力，有圣雄甘地（印度政治领袖）一样坚韧的意志力"。[2]

> "我最大的灵感来自卡尼曼和特沃斯基。"
>
> ——理查德·H. 泰勒，引自伊琳娜·哈罗宁："学术英雄：
> 理查德·H. 泰勒"，"决策中"博客

学科概览

尽管经济学家们早就知道理性选择理论受到的批评，[3] 理性选择理论的优势却在于它允许经济学家对经济行为做出明晰的预测。许多预测得到了经验证据（可通过观察验证的证据）的证实，例如当物价上涨时购买力降低，而当薪酬上涨时，人们会多工作，这表明该模型对于群体的长期预测是大致准确的。

美国诺贝尔经济学奖获得者赫伯特·西蒙*曾挑战过完全理性假说，他在 20 世纪四五十年代发表的几篇文章中提出，人的行为受心理因素制约，做不到完全理性。然而，泰勒认为，"西蒙对经济学的影响不大。原因是……他没有考虑系统性偏差。"[4] 也就是说西蒙并没能够证明人们的实际行为会一直与理性选择理论预测的行为相反。凯莫勒和罗文斯坦支持泰勒的观点，认为西蒙的研究"引起了人们的注意，但没有从根本上改变经济学的方向"。[5]

学术渊源

泰勒洞察到"存在可预测的认知偏差"。[6] 这意味着，有时人们可能会持续做出"非理性"的，不符合理性选择理论标准的行为。

泰勒这一思想源于对丹尼尔·卡尼曼和阿莫斯·特沃斯基在 20 世纪 70 年代科研成果的研究。在那十年间，卡尼曼和特沃斯基

发表了一系列关于人类决策的开创性论文。特沃斯基于 1996 年去世，他的合作者卡尼曼于 2002 年获得了诺贝尔经济学奖，获奖理由是他"把心理学的研究成果与经济学融合在一起，特别是对在不确定状态下人们如何作出判断和决策方面的研究"。[7] 1974 年两人在《科学》* 杂志上发表了论文"不确定状态下的判断：启发和偏见"，产生很大影响。该论文认为人们经常依赖认知捷径做出判断和决策，这个认知捷径被他们称为"启发"*。其中"可得性启发"* 是指人们通常依赖于大脑中立即涌现的事例做出判断。采用这种启发的人可能会高估心脏病发作死亡的风险，原因在于即使统计数据表明心脏病发作造成死亡的概率较低，他们也可以随时联想到有心脏病的朋友。

卡尼曼和特沃斯基 1979 年在《计量经济学》* 期刊上发表了另一篇重要论文"前景理论"*。他们发现面对收获或损失人们处理金钱的方式不同。例如掷硬币，如果掷到正面赢 20 美元，掷到反面输 20 美元。大多数人都不愿接受这种赌博，因为他们的实验对象虽然喜欢赢钱，但更厌恶输钱，这一现象被称为"损失厌恶"*。这与新古典主义经济学的预测相矛盾。新古典主义经济学假设人们会以同样的方式对待收益和损失。可得性启发和损失厌恶以及许多其他启发和偏见表明人们可能会表现出系统的"非理性"行为。

20 世纪 80 年代，泰勒在权威期刊《经济展望杂志》* 上开设了一个名为"反常现象"的专栏，收集有关行为偏见的案例。[8] 该专栏为泰勒提供了一个虽然很小但极具影响力的平台，向主流经济学宣传行为经济学这一新领域的研究成果。卡尼曼认为"('反常现象'专栏）开辟了行为经济学这个新领域……值得推崇"。[9]

1. 科林·凯莫勒和乔治·罗文斯坦："行为经济学：过去、现在和未来"，科林·凯莫勒等编，《行为经济学研究进展》，新泽西州普林斯顿：普利斯顿大学出版社，2003 年。

2. 理查德·H.泰勒和卡斯·R.桑斯坦：《助推：如何做出有关健康、财富和幸福的更优决策》，纽约：耶鲁大学出版社，2008 年，第 6 页。

3. 加里·贝克尔："非理性行为和经济理论"，《政治经济学杂志》第 70 卷，1962年第 1 期，第 1—13 页。

4. 理查德·H.泰勒："你需要助推吗？"，《耶鲁视点》，2009 年 11 月 4 日，登录日期 2015 年 9 月 4 日，http://insights.com.yale.edu/insights/do-you-need-nudge。

5. 凯莫勒和罗文斯坦："行为经济学：过去、现在和未来"，第 5 页。

6. 泰勒："你需要助推吗？"。

7. "2002 年诺贝尔经济学奖"，诺贝尔奖官网，登录日期 2015 年 9 月 4 日，http://www.nobelprize.org/nobel_prizes/economic-sciences/laureates/2002/。

8. 理查德·H.泰勒主持的"反常现象"专栏，登录日期 2015 年 9 月 4 日，http://faculty.chicagobooth.edu/Richard.Thaler/research/anomalies.html。

9. 格里高利·卡普："简介：理查德·H.泰勒，芝加哥大学布斯商学院教授"，《芝加哥论坛报》，2012 年 4 月 30 日，登录日期 2015 年 9 月 4 日，http://articles.chicagotribune.com/2012-04-30/business/ct-biz-0430-executive-profile-thaler-20120430_1_economics-daniel-kahneman-cost-fallacy。

3 主导命题

要点 🔑

- 理性选择理论认为人们在经济上的决策是理性的。《助推》源于对理性选择理论的批判，认为它不足以解释许多人类经济行为。

- 行为经济学研究表明，人们经常在决策中犯"非理性"错误。

- 《助推》综合了数百项研究，认为行为经济学理论可以对人类行为做出更现实的解读。

核心问题

泰勒和桑斯坦写作《助推》的缘起是因为他们认为新古典主义经济学的理性选择模型（人们根据完全的信息做出理性的决策）不足以解释许多人类经济行为，而行为经济学理论则能够更现实地解释人类决策行为。

理查德·H. 泰勒在 20 世纪 70 年代博士学习期间接受过新古典主义经济学教育。他认为理性选择理论的确是人们应该如何行动的理想模型，但它无法准确解读现实世界中的真实行为。泰勒曾说："如果你想要单一的、统一的经济行为理论，我们已经有了，利己的、理性的经济人假设就是最好的选择……，但如果你不是在为人们决策提供建议，而是试图预测他们实际上会怎样做，那么问题就出现了。"[1]

充分描述完全理性的含义或许可以解除泰勒对理性行为理论的质疑。在理性选择理论的世界中人们不会犯错。他们不会冲动购物而导致后悔，[2] 他们不会在想要戒烟时抽烟，[3] 他们会坚持节食从不中途放弃，[4] 他们不会背负负担不起的贷款，[5] 他们也不会盲目自信冒险开公司。[6] 此外，他们还对框架效应有天然的免疫力。[7] 例如，一个汉堡无论标识为脂肪含量90%或非脂肪含量10%，都不会对他们产生影响。即便有87%的人认为注册器官捐献是正确的做法，这类社会规范也不会影响他们的判断。[8] 他们的头脑不易受到启发和损失厌恶（人们更在意避免损失而不是获得收益的倾向）这类偏见的影响，也不受可得性启发*（认知经验法则，指人们依靠最先想到的事例作为判断依据）的影响。理性参与者决策时不需要帮助，因为他们在任何时候都会做出最优决定。

> "人们在许多情况下做出了非常糟糕的决定。如果他们足够重视，拥有完备的信息、完美的认知能力和绝对的自控力，他们就不会做出那样的决定。"
>
> —— 理查德·H. 泰勒和卡斯·R. 桑斯坦：
> 《助推：如何做出有关健康、财富和幸福的更优决策》

参与者

泰勒和桑斯坦写《助推》之前，行为经济学已经记录了大量的心理学证据，表明人们确实经常表现出那些在理性选择理论看来"非理性"的经济行为。

在金融领域，泰勒和经济学家沃纳·德·邦特*发现，认知偏差会影响股票市场的运作。[9] 1997年，美国经济学家大卫·莱布森*提出了一个重要的模型，他认为自控力较差的人不太可能为退休生活储蓄。[10] 2001年，美国经济学家布里吉特·马德里安*和丹尼斯·谢伊*证明，改变默认规则能够影响重要经济行为。他们发现，将一些员工自动纳入某项养老金计划，而不愿意参加的员工选择退出，可以大大提高该计划的参与率。[11] 2008 年，《助推》出版的当年，哈佛大学约翰·贝西尔斯教授 * 及其同事发现在某些情况下，市场不一定能使人采取理性行动，这与新古典主义经济学的假设相反。[12]

当代论战

《助推》综合了几十年来数百篇学术论文研究成果。书中讨论了各个时代学者对人类行为的研究，强调了行为经济学的悠久历史和跨学科性质。

尽管心理学研究的实验证据已经被纳入主流经济学，但是经济学家对这些证据所代表的含义的理解并不一致。最近，一本本科经济学教科书中称："行为经济学研究表明，新古典主义经济学的理性决策公理经不起逻辑、经验或社会需求的检验。"[13] 另一本教科书则对此持怀疑态度，认为"市场倾向于奖励理性行为，同时惩罚非理性行为。即便许多市场参与者的行为缺乏理性，仍然是那些表现得足够理性的人对价格和结果的影响最大"。[14] 换句话说，非理性的个体行为可能不会对整个群体产生重要影响。

最后，行为经济学家科林·凯莫勒和乔治·罗文斯坦提供了一个平衡的观点，他们认为"行为经济学的核心在于一种信念，即用于经济分析的心理学基础越走向实用，就越能促进经济学本身的进步——发展理论观点，更好地预测经济现象，提出更好的政策建议。这种信念并不意味着完全否定新古典主义经济学思想"。[15]

1. 理查德·H.泰勒："何时会有一个统一的'行为'经济理论？"，选自"你的领域里害怕被问到问题是什么？"，《边缘》，2014年3月28日，登录日期2015年9月4日，http://edge.org/conversation/whats-the-question-about-your-field-that-you-dread-being-asked#25056。

2. 理查德·H.泰勒和卡斯·R.桑斯坦：《助推：如何做出有关健康、财富和幸福的更优决策》，纽约：耶鲁大学出版社，2008年，第51页。

3. 泰勒和桑斯坦：《助推》，第44页。

4. 泰勒和桑斯坦：《助推》，第7页。

5. 泰勒和桑斯坦：《助推》，第134页。

6. 泰勒和桑斯坦：《助推》，第32页。

7. 泰勒和桑斯坦：《助推》，第36页。

8. 泰勒和桑斯坦：《助推》，第182页。

9. 沃纳·德·邦特和理查德·H.泰勒："股票市场是否反应过度了？"，《金融杂志》第40卷，1985年第3期，第793—805页。

10. 大卫·莱布森："金蛋和双曲线贴现"，《经济学季刊》第112卷，1997年第2期，第443—478页。

11. 布里吉特·马德里安和丹尼斯·谢伊："建议的力量：论加入401（k）养老金计划与储蓄行为中的惰性"，《经济学季刊》第116卷，2001年第4期，第1149—1187页。

12. 约翰·贝西尔斯等："揭示偏好"，《公共经济学杂志》第92卷，2008年，第1787—1794页。

13. 涅瓦·古德温等：《语境中的微观经济学》第三版，阿宾登：劳特利奇出版社，2013年，第155页。

14. 哈尔·瓦里安：《中级微观经济学》第八版，纽约：W.W.诺顿出版社，2009年，第579页。

15. 科林·科莫勒和乔治·罗文斯坦："行为经济学：过去、现在和未来"，科林·凯莫勒等编，《行为经济学研究进展》，新泽西州普林斯顿：普林斯顿大学出版社，2003年。

4 作者贡献

要点 🔑

- 泰勒和桑斯坦在《助推》中的主要观点是，政府应该在尊重民众自由选择权的同时帮助他们做出更优决策。

- 协调上述两者之间的矛盾是《助推》的主要见解之一。

- 《助推》提出的"自由主义的温和专制主义"理念——一种建立在自由选择（自由主义）和善意干预（温和专制主义）基础上的思想——主要基于 2003 年泰勒、桑斯坦和同时代其他学者的研究成果。

作者目标

泰勒和桑斯坦在《助推：如何做出有关健康、财富和幸福的更优决策》一书的开篇章节中提到，人们的决策往往受到心理因素的影响。他们不但引用了大量的证据，还补充了自己观察到的非理性经济行为和一些趣闻轶事，来表明心理因素会导致人们做出糟糕的决策。

泰勒和桑斯坦提出了政府干预的观点，并解释了其含义。他们认为政府应该利用行为经济学理论来帮助民众做出更明智的决策，从而改善他们的生活。但泰勒和桑斯坦也明确指出，政府的干预不应带有强迫性。为此，他们援引了经济学家米尔顿·弗里德曼的思想作为理论依据。弗里德曼认为人们应该有权"自由选择"。[1] 泰勒和桑斯坦将这种政治哲学称为"自由主义的温和专制主义"。

　　《助推》提倡通过有限的政府干预来改善个人决策效果，这个观点并非完全新颖——行为经济学家科林·凯莫勒和他的同事们在 2003 年提出了类似的观点。[2] 然而，《助推》的巨大成功在于它用通俗易懂的语言向普通读者展示了"温和专制主义"的理念，同时运用大量的科学证据予以佐证。

> "我们主张通过私营企业和政府的自觉努力，引导人们做出改善他们生活的选择。"
>
> —— 理查德·H. 泰勒和卡斯·R. 桑斯坦:
> 《助推: 如何做出有关健康、财富和幸福的更优决策》

研究方法

　　《助推》引用了数百项科学研究成果证明心理因素会对决策产生负面影响，从而为政府干预提供了理论依据。他们在行为经济学和法学方面的专业知识背景使得该书论点令人信服。泰勒是行为经济学的奠基人，自 20 世纪 80 年代以来，他在《经济展望杂志》开设"反常现象"专栏，系统地收集了理性行为偏差的事例。[3] 桑斯坦的研究成果极具影响力，他研究行为经济学的原理在法学领域的应用，解释人们与法律体系的互动。他对政府管理的专业知识和政治理念为《助推》一书贡献了清晰的政府干预框架。

　　2003 年，泰勒和桑斯坦发表了论文《自由主义的温和专制主义不是矛盾修辞法》，首次提出了政府干预的观点。[4] 这篇论文的题目突显出一对显而易见的矛盾。自由主义是一种强调个人自由、反对政府监督的政治哲学。而温和专制主义就像禁止孩子吃快餐的父母那样，认为对他人有利就替他们做出决定。泰勒和桑斯坦微妙地调和了这对矛盾。他们建议政府在尊重民众自由选择权的前提下，采取干预措施以帮助民众做出更明智的决策。他们以一个公司为例，该公司鼓励员工为退休以后的生活储蓄。[5]公司没有要求员工参加养老金计划，而是假设他们愿意参加，并通过默认选项将所有员工纳入了养老金计划，而那些不想参加的员工可以额外选择退出。人们通常会倾向于采用默认选项，这使得员工储蓄率上升，而那些不想参加养老金计划的员工的意愿也能被满足。

时代贡献

泰勒和桑斯坦在五年后出版的《助推》里延续了自由主义的温和专制主义的观点，但是在不同的语境中予以全新诠释。《助推》以美国政治为背景，更明确地将自由主义的温和专制主义理念推销给美国读者。他们认为"社会没有必要两极分化"，他们的提议可能"成为一个切实可行的中间地带"[6]，并可能成为"真正的第三条道路"[7]；它既能吸引民主党，也能吸引共和党（也就是说，能吸引不同的政治派别）。

泰勒和桑斯坦并不是唯一提出这种观点的行为经济学家。在他们提出"自由主义的温和专制主义"概念的 2003 年，行为经济学家科林·凯莫勒及其同事也提出了一个"不对称家长式作风"的说法。[8]这两种理念本质上是相同的，说明它们源自同一个学派。不过，凯莫勒和他的同事们在阐述"不对称家长式作风"在政治上的潜在应用时更为直接。他们的论文题目"保守主义人士也能接受的规制"*隐含的意思是，由于自由党派往往对政府干预持更开放的态度，因此如果要让"助推"式干预被广泛接受，那么最需要说服的是保守党派。

1. 理查德·H. 泰勒和卡斯·R. 桑斯坦:《助推:如何做出有关健康、财富和幸福的更优决策》,纽约:耶鲁大学出版社,2008 年,第 5 页。

2. 科林·凯莫勒等:"保守主义人士也能接受的规制:行为经济学与'不对称家长式作风'的案例评论",《宾夕法尼亚大学法律评论》第 151 卷,2003 年第 3 期,第 1211—1254 页。

3. 理查德·H. 泰勒主持的"反常现象"专栏,登录日期 2015 年 9 月 4 日,http://faculty.chicagobooth.edu/Richard.Thaler/research/anomalies.html。

4. 理查德·H. 泰勒和卡斯·R. 桑斯坦:"自由主义的温和专制主义不是矛盾修辞法",《芝加哥大学法律评论》第 70 卷,2003 年第 4 期,第 1159—1202 页。

5. 泰勒和桑斯坦:《助推》,第 109 页。

6. 泰勒和桑斯坦:《助推》,第 252 页。

7. 泰勒和桑斯坦:《助推》,第 252 页。

8. 凯莫勒等:"保守主义人士也能接受的规制"。

第二部分：学术思想

5 思想主脉

要点 🔑

- 《助推》有两个主题：环境如何影响决策，以及政府如何在不限制选择自由的情况下调整环境，以帮助民众做出更优决策。

- 泰勒和桑斯坦的主要观点是，在人们进行判断时，政府应该"助推"人们做出更优决策。

- 作者通过在金融、卫生和环境等领域的具体助推事例，强调了助推观点在政策中的适用性。

核心主题

《助推》是一本关于人类决策的著作。在该书中，泰勒和桑斯坦探讨了有关助推的两大主题：

- 环境如何影响决策
- 政府如何在不限制人们选择自由的情况下，通过调整环境来帮助人们做出更优决策。

《助推》的开篇描述了影响决策的心理因素，包括启发（认知经验法则）和偏见（倾向于接受对信息的某种解释）、情绪和诱惑、社会压力及认知能力（充分利用智力的能力）的限制。

泰勒和桑斯坦认为，由于存在这些因素，决策环境往往会导致人们做出错误的决定。泰勒和桑斯坦提出的解决方案是，政府在不禁止任何选项的情况下，设计选择环境，这样民众就更有可能根据自己的最佳利益采取行动。他们将这种方式称之为"助推"。

> "助推……以可预见的方式改变人们的行为，不禁止任何选项，不显著改变他们的经济动机。助推式的干预必须不需要什么成本就能予以避免……把水果放在与目光平齐的地方是一种助推，但禁止垃圾食品则不是。"
>
> ——理查德·H. 泰勒和卡斯·R. 桑斯坦：
> 《助推：如何做出有关健康、财富和幸福的更优决策》

思想探究

《助推》的主要论点是，人们做决定时所处的环境会影响他们的选择。作者举了一个在线政府项目的例子，该项目要求老年人从47种不同的处方药方案中选择一种。[1] 这个项目设计得过于复杂，很难做出最佳选择。通过设计决策环境达到影响行为的目的就是泰勒和桑斯坦所说的"选择架构"。[2] 他们认为，政府应该创建更好的选择架构，以帮助民众做出明智的决策。同时，他们也强调这种帮助不是胁迫，政府不应剥夺他们的选择自由。

泰勒和桑斯坦所说的"助推"是指在不禁止任何选项的情况下，为鼓励某种行为而改变选择架构。用他们的话来说，"助推……以可预见的方式改变人们的行为，而不禁止任何选项，不显著改变他们的经济动机。"[3] 这样的例子随处可见：引导司机到达目的地的卫星导航系统，鼓励人们走楼梯不乘电梯的标志，利用社会规范来鼓励某个行为的声明（如"大多数人按时交税"），以及政府发布的营养指南等。又如，在线药物处方网站根据患者以前的处方情况自动安排用药方案，但同时也提供其他方案供选择。[4] 这也是有效的助推。

在《助推》中，泰勒和桑斯坦通过趣闻轶事和科学实验证据来阐述他们的观点。他们还列举了许多具体的、实用的例子，以说明政府和企业可以利用"助推"改善人们的决策。

一个例子是美国的"明日储蓄"项目。[5] 该项目受到行为经济学理论研究的推动，认为人们的拖延行为阻碍了他们对退休计划的安排。项目要求公司员工明确未来工资中一定的百分比用作养老基金。因此，当他们加薪时，养老基金也会自动同比增长。这就解决了惰性（不作为）问题，因为员工不需要在每次加薪时主动更新他们的养老储蓄数额。

另一个例子是器官捐赠。尽管调查显示许多人支持器官捐赠，但很少有人注册成为器官捐赠者。泰勒和桑斯坦认为，注册必需的繁复程序阻碍了人们的行动。他们提出"强制选择"可以缩小意愿与行动之间的差距。[6] 当民众与政府部门打交道时可以通过助推手段鼓励人们做出选择，比如司机在申请驾照的时候，必须勾选一个方框表达是否愿意捐赠器官。

还有能源效率的例子。这个领域最大的问题是大多数消费者对能源效率的情况不了解。《助推》强调了信息披露法在这方面发挥的作用。例如，某项法律要求汽车公司张贴的汽车油耗标签采用醒目的大字体。[7] 这个助推手段将促使部分有节能意识的消费者购买更节能的汽车。

语言表述

《助推》是一部通俗易懂的经济学著作，它同时面向普通读者、学者和决策者。泰勒和桑斯坦通过一些简单风趣的事例，以及科学研究中的量化证据来佐证自己的观点。该书最后还对美国如何在多个领域应用"助推"思想提出了具体建议。

　　《助推》提出了三个新概念："助推"、"选择架构"和"自由主义的温和专制主义"。前两个概念指通过调整决策环境来鼓励某些行为的方式。最后一个概念描述了助推背后的哲学，调和了政府尊重个人选择自由和家长式代言人的矛盾。这三个术语在学术界和政界都为人们所熟知，彰显了该书巨大的影响力。

---

1. 理查德·H. 泰勒和卡斯·R. 桑斯坦：《助推：如何做出有关健康、财富和幸福的更优决策》，纽约：耶鲁大学出版社，2008年，第5页。
2. 泰勒和桑斯坦：《助推》，第3页。
3. 泰勒和桑斯坦：《助推》，第6页。
4. 泰勒和桑斯坦：《助推》，第172页。
5. 泰勒和桑斯坦：《助推》，第113页。
6. 泰勒和桑斯坦：《助推》，第180页。
7. 泰勒和桑斯坦：《助推》，第191页。

6 思想支脉

要点 🗝

- 《助推》提到两个次要观点：人们做决策时采用直觉思维（快速的和本能的）系统和理性思维（有意识的和经过计算的）系统＊；事实上私营部门的助推策略经常对民众产生影响。

- 上述两个观点解释了助推的工作机制，并含蓄地强调了助推潜在的"黑暗面"。

- 《助推》认为即使政府不打算做出助推式干涉，但事实上它已经通过现有的选择架构在这样做了，这个观点可以用来反驳该书后来受到的某些批评。

其他思想

《助推》中有两个次要观点：

- 人们做决策时采用直觉思维系统和理性思维系统；
- 无论政府是否干预民众，他们在日常生活中都不断地受到助推的影响。

为了帮助读者理解助推的工作机制，《助推》开篇就对直觉思维系统和理性思维系统进行了探讨。泰勒和桑斯坦讨论了心理学和神经科学对人类大脑功能的研究。大脑采用两种方式工作：一种是快速的、本能的直觉思维系统，另一种是较慢的、更理性的理性思维系统。[1] 泰勒和桑斯坦在书中谈到的许多助推行为似乎都是针对直觉思维系统设计的，也就是说，助推行为应该无意识地引导民众而非鼓励他们更多地反思自己的选择。

事实上，在现实世界中民众的日常生活一直在受助推影响。"助推"以广告和销售技巧的形式普遍存在。虽然《助推》只建议推行旨在改善人类福祉的"善意助推"，但很容易令人联想到的潜台词是也存在着"恶意助推"，它们鼓励不健康的生活习惯或浪费性消费。

> "（助推）是常态。我们一直受助推影响。夏娃和蛇影响了亚当。几千年来，宗教一直影响着我们的行为。各种营销方式和广告影响消费者。我们会被推向善或被推向恶……助推不是我们发明的。"
>
> —— 理查德·H.泰勒："你需要助推吗？"，《耶鲁视点》

思想探究

《助推》用"经济人"与"社会人"的概念来对应新古典主义经济学和行为经济学在描述人类行为上的差异——前者代表影响西方经济政策的主流的、正统的方法，后者则融合了心理学和经济学的研究。"经济人"是指理性选择理论中完美的"理性人"。"社会人"是真实世界的人，时常做出不理性的决策。《助推》开篇就将"经济人"和"社会人"的概念与心理学理论中的"直觉"和"理性"思维系统关联起来。[2] 以色列心理学家丹尼尔·卡尼曼在他的《思考，快与慢》[3] 一书中，将直觉思维系统和理性思维系统分别称作系统1和系统2，并对它们进行了更详细的阐述。

直觉思维系统是快速的、本能的。它受感觉、习惯和环境中的触发因素驱动，需要极少甚至不需要任何认知参与。这就是"社会人"的思维方式。例如：

• 不经过思考就知道 2+2 等于几；
• 从某人的语调和肢体语言立刻判断出他在生气；

- 毫不费力地理解母语中的短句。

理性思维系统是深思熟虑的、理性的。它受价值、知识和意图驱动，需要认知参与。这就是"经济人"的思维方式。例如：

- 计算 391×624；

- 在大学里选专业和课程；

- 慢慢地、仔细地听懂外语。

助推通常通过直觉思维系统来改变人的行为，因此它能够影响社会人（使用直觉思维系统的人）而无法影响经济人（不使用直觉思维系统的人）。例如，将大多数人的喜好作为默认规则，用更具吸引力的方式设计选项，简化复杂的选项使之更易懂。所有这些助推都减轻了认知负担，正如《助推》所说的那样，"使人们的选择变得更容易。"[4]

《助推》的另一个观点是，在我们的日常生活中，"助推"无处不在。这其中的潜台词是，这些"助推"可能并没有把公众的最大利益放在心上。例如，有一篇书评将助推称为"一个营销人员的梦想"。[5] 几十年来，销售和广告一直在使用《助推》中描述的一些技巧，比如产品布置和名人代言。美国苹果公司的 iBeacon 产品就是将助推理念应用到现代广告中的一个例子。记者尼亚·齐普金描述了在美国的一些商场，iBeacon 技术如何通过顾客的智能手机锁定他们在商场里的行踪，甚至定位到他们在过道所站的位置。[6] 这个技术将顾客视线范围内的产品销售信息推送到顾客的手机上，为顾客提供个性化购物体验。

被忽视之处

《助推》中提出的一个巧妙的论据是，即便政府不打算助推民众，实际上却已经在这么做了。也就是说"选择架构及其影响是不可避免的"。[7]

批评人士忽视了这一观点。他们批评《助推》提倡的过于家长式的作风——对民众的生活进行过多的善意干预。桑斯坦对此回应道，"不管政府是否有意助推，政府网站发布信息，与百姓交流沟通，经营自助餐厅，维护市民处理事务的公共场所，无论何时它都在助推。"[8] 他认为现有的选择架构中不存在"中立"这一默认设置。政府已经通过其现有机构以各种方式在影响民众的行为。

桑斯坦的观点暗示，正因如此，政府应该调整那些机构，使之助推民众（使他们觉得像是自己做出的判断那样）朝着更好的方向前进。桑斯坦后来在他的著作《简化：政府的未来》[9] 中作了进一步阐述。该书探讨了他在担任白宫信息与法规事务办公室主任三年任期内的工作经历。他在书中强调应简化现有政府形式和结构以提高其效率的重要性。

---

1. 理查德·H.泰勒和卡斯·R.桑斯坦：《助推：如何做出有关健康、财富和幸福的更优决策》，纽约：耶鲁大学出版社，2008年，第19页。

2. 泰勒和桑斯坦：《助推》，第19页。

3. 丹尼尔·卡尼曼：《思考，快与慢》，纽约：法勒，斯特劳斯与吉鲁出版社，2011年。

4. 泰勒和桑斯坦：《助推》，第5页。

5. 杰里米·沃尔德伦："这都是为了你好"，《纽约书评》，2014年10月9日，登录日期2015年9月4日，http://www.nybooks.com/articles/archives/2014/oct/09/cass-

sunstein-its-all-your-own-good/。

6. 尼亚·齐普金:"注意了,苹果的消费者们:你们被跟踪了",2013 年 12 月 6 日,登录日期 2015 年 9 月 4 日,http://www.entrepreneur.com/article/230275。

7. 泰勒和桑斯坦:《助推》,第 72 页。

8. 卡斯·R.桑斯坦:"助推受到反对——但它从来不是要解决所有问题",《卫报》,2014 年 4 月 24 日,登录日期 2015 年 9 月 4 日,http://www.theguardian.com/commentisfree/2014/apr/24/nudge-backlash-free-society-dignity-coercion。

9. 卡斯·R.桑斯坦:《简化:政府的未来》,纽约:西蒙与舒斯特出版社,2013 年。

7 历史成就

要点 ⚷—

- 《助推》受到了公众、学者和决策者的好评。
- 《助推》的成功归功于大量的科学实验证据，众多真实的助推事例，及其出版时机。
- 虽然助推手段可以改善决策，但也具有局限性，无法应对重大的社会挑战。

观点评价

《助推》提出了一个令人信服的观点：政府应该"助推"其民众做出更好的决策。该书总结了几十年来行为经济学和心理学的研究成果，写作风格通俗易懂，深受公众、学者和决策者的欢迎，取得了巨大的成功。

《助推》关于人类决策的观点看上去更现实，与新古典主义经济学更为抽象和理论性的假设形成鲜明对比。曾有书评指出《助推》的成功可能还因为它出版于 2008 年年中，当时正值金融危机，新古典主义经济学因未能预测到此次危机而遭到了许多质疑。[1]

在学术界，《助推》提出的"选择架构"和"助推"思想很快被其他对行为改变感兴趣的学科所采纳。例如，公共卫生研究者为了改善大众的健康，已经在研究是否可以通过助推手段减少吸烟、肥胖和运动不足等问题。[2] 市场营销人员运用助推方式影响消费者的行为，[3] 政治学家们也在研究是否能够通过助推鼓励投票等公民行为。[4]

当时的成就

《助推》提出的轻触式政府监管理念和看似常识性的政策解决方案吸引了众多读者。[5]该书不仅成了畅销书,更影响了现实世界的决策。在英国,助推被视为特别有吸引力的政策手段,部分原因是当时正值英国政府为应对2008年金融危机而削减支出,而施行这种政策手段的成本相对较低。[6]《助推》的观点很快被右翼保守党采纳。该书出版三个月后,保守党议员、未来的财政大臣乔治·奥斯本*在《卫报》上称赞了《助推》。[7]2010年,时任英国首相的保守党领袖戴维·卡梅伦创建了全球第一个助推小组,以促进政府官员落实该书理念。助推小组成立五年内发表了多篇报告,记录了其在税收、失业、慈善等不同领域的政策干预,进一步扩大了该书的影响力。[8]

《助推》的成功还催生了美国社会与行为科学团队。2015年9月,美国总统贝拉克·奥巴马*签署行政命令,正式成立社会与行为科学团队。这份行政命令指出"行为科学和心理学对人类决策和行动的研究可以用来设计政府政策,从而更好地为美国人民服务"。[9]这份行政命令还附带了一份报告,描述了该团队最近进行的助推活动。他们的成功举措包括给低收入学生发送个性化短信,提高了该群体的大学入学率;简化政府债务催收信,使得在线支付用户增多;要求政府采购供应商进行网上申请时,在表格上方签名(以增加诚信度),此举提高了供应商提供的销售数据的准确性。[10]

局限性

《助推》的一个重要优势在于"选择架构"和"助推"具有普适性。因为这与人们的基本决策过程有关，所以该书的观点适用于不同国家和不同环境。

尽管如此，"助推"仍有一个很大的局限性，那就是它必须"易被摆脱并且摆脱成本低廉"。[11] 助推不允许使用税收和监管等更传统的政策工具。2009 年，英国政治家埃德·米利班德 * 强调了这一局限性。他批评英国在陷入衰退之际推出助推政策的想法。他认为"在金融危机爆发前的几个月……《助推》很时髦。《助推》是说政府不需要去做大事……人们已不再谈论《助推》了"。[12] 米利班德后来成为中左派政党工党 * 的领袖。

然而，米利班德对《助推》只会风行一时的评价无疑是错误的，因为此后很多年该书继续对英国和美国的政策产生影响。但是，米利班德有一点可能是正确的，即在面对经济衰退等重大挑战时，助推无法与传统政策工具媲美。《助推》建议渐进式的政策调整。与此形成鲜明对比的是，美国政府为应对 2008 年金融危机而拨出 8 310 亿美元刺激经济。按照《助推》中的原则，这种干预本应被禁止，而其他针对肥胖和气候变化等挑战的政府大规模应对措施也同样应该被禁止。

---

1. 乔尔·安德森："评论《助推：如何做出有关健康、财富和幸福的更优决策》"，

《经济学与哲学》第26卷，2010年第3期，第369—376页。

2. 特丽萨·马图等："审视助推：助推能改善人口健康吗？"，《英国医学杂志》第342卷，2011年。

3. 丹尼尔·G.戈德斯坦等："把你的客户推向更好的选择"，《哈佛商业评论》，2008年12月，登录日期2015年9月4日，https://hbr.org/2008/12/nudge-your-customers-toward-better-choices。

4. 大卫·W.尼克尔森和托德·罗杰斯："你有投票计划吗？实施意向、选民投票率和有机计划制定"，《心理科学》第21卷，2001年第2期，第194—199页。

5. 本杰明·M.弗里德曼："引导力"，《纽约时报》，2008年8月22日，登录日期2015年9月5日，http://www.nytimes.com/2008/08/24/books/review/Friedman-t.html?pagewanted=all&_r=0。

6. 戴维·卡梅伦："谈下一代的政府"，TED，2010年2月，登录日期2015年9月4日，http://www.ted.com/talks/david_cameron?language=en。

7. 乔治·奥斯本："助推、助推，胜利、胜利"，《卫报》，2008年7月14日，登录日期2015年9月4日，http://theguardian.com/commentisfree/2008/jul/14/conservatives.economy。

8. 行为洞察团队："行为洞察团队2013—2015年更新报告"，登录日期2015年9月4日，http://behaviouralinsights.co.uk/wp-content/uploads/2015/07/BIT_Update-Report-Final-2013-2015.pdf。

9. "行政命令——使用行为洞察科学更好地为美国人民服务"，白宫新闻秘书办公室，2015年9月15日，登录日期2015年9月30日，https://www.whitehouse.gov/the-press-office/2015/09/15/executive-order-using-behavioral-science-insights-better-serve-american。

10. 社会与行为科学团队："社会与行为科学团队年度报告"，总统国家科学技术委员会执行办公室，2015年9月，登录日期2015年9月30日，https://www.whitehouse.gov/sites/default/files/microsites/ostp/sbst_2015_annual_report_final_9_14_15.pdf。

11. 理查德·H.泰勒和卡斯·R.桑斯坦：《助推：如何做出有关健康、财富和幸福的更优决策》，纽约：耶鲁大学出版社，2008年，第6页。

12. 安德鲁·斯派洛："费边会议——现场报道"，《卫报》，2009年1月17日，登录日期2015年9月4日，http://theguardian.com/politics/blog/2009/jan/17/fabian-conference-blog。

8 著作地位

要点 🔑

- 在整个学术生涯中，泰勒和桑斯坦坚持采用心理学和行为经济学理论来解读人类决策。

- 尽管泰勒和桑斯坦在写《助推》之前就已在学界享有盛誉，但该书极大地提高了他们的知名度。《助推》至今仍是他们的最高成就。

- 《助推》将行为经济学研究推向全球，是泰勒的巅峰之作。

定位

2008 年《助推》出版时，泰勒和桑斯坦两人都已在学术界工作了三十年。他们在芝加哥大学担任教授职务，研究行为经济学原理在金融和法律领域的应用，他们的学术著作均被广泛引用。尽管二位作者已经成绩斐然，《助推》仍是他们在职业生涯中取得的最大成就。该书成为国际知名畅销书，直接影响了一些世界最发达国家的政府决策，并被多个学科高度引用。

《助推》体现了作者长期以来用行为经济学和心理学理论改善人类决策的兴趣。1998 年，他们与美国法学教授克里斯汀·焦尔斯*合作阐述了行为经济学如何为法律和政治提供更实际的理论基础。[1] 2003 年，他们在《芝加哥大学法律评论》上发表的一篇文章中，描述了自由主义的温和专制主义如何影响政府决策。[2] 这篇名为"自由主义的温和专制主义不是矛盾修辞法"的论文得出的结论是，他们的思想可以为"重新思考私法和公法的很多领域提供基础"。[3]

后来，为了深度阐述他们的观点，泰勒和桑斯坦将那篇 44 页的论文扩展成了一部293页的著作，即《助推》。该书从多个方面充实了原来的内容，对相关心理学研究的描述更完整，这些研究为他们探讨人类决策提供了依据。他们列举了更多"助推"事例，阐述了助推思想对美国政治的适用性。该书通俗易懂，也吸引了大量普通读者。

> "自由主义的温和专制主义为理解和反思当代法律提供了基础，包括那些涉及工作福利、消费者保护和家庭的法律。"
>
> ——理查德·H.泰勒和卡斯·R.桑斯坦：
> "自由主义的温和专制主义不是矛盾修辞法"，《芝加哥大学评论》

整合

泰勒的研究整体上是连贯的，他一直在阐述行为经济学方面的问题。与泰勒不同，桑斯坦的学术兴趣广泛，写作主题不是那么统一。他发表最多的是关于法律和国家治理方面的论著，同时也涉及动物权利、阴谋论和政治极端主义等深奥话题。桑斯坦以多产闻名——截至2015年，他发表专著、论文和媒体评论等出版物约500种。

《助推》一书将行为经济学推向全球，成为泰勒一生成就的顶峰。他在该领域发表了许多最重要的论文。20世纪80年代和90年代，泰勒在《经济展望杂志》开设"反常现象"专栏，使之成为向主流经济学派介绍行为经济学研究成果的平台。因此，诺贝尔奖得主、心理学家丹尼尔·卡尼曼称泰勒是"行为经济学真正的缔造者"。[4]《助推》的热销及其发挥的影响力佐证了行为经济学的发展道路：从最初被众多经济学家无视[5]发展到一个受人尊敬的学科，它为研究人类行为提供了重要的见解。

《助推》也是桑斯坦对其研究工作的有效总结，他探讨了行为经济学如何为法律和国家治理提供依据。"助推"通常强调对现有政策进行渐进式的、针对具体案例的修改，这与桑斯坦"司法极简主义"的主张一致。司法极简主义是一种法律哲学，它倾向于个案裁决，而不是对宪法性法律进行大肆修改。

意义

在《助推》出版前，就有许多学者预测泰勒很有可能成为未来的诺贝尔经济学奖得主。[6]（泰勒于 2017 年获得诺贝尔经济学奖——译者加。）桑斯坦是全球被引用率最高的法学家之一，也是奥巴马政府高官，曾担任白宫信息与法规事务办公室主任，任期三年。尽管两位作者此前已经取得了卓越成就，《助推》的成功将他们进一步推向世界。

《助推》在现实世界最引人注目的成效是它对全球政策制定的影响。"轻触监管"的理念强烈吸引了英国保守党。2010 年，《助推》出版仅两年之后，英国首相戴维·卡梅伦将该书的理念付诸实践，在保守党领导的政府中创建了全球第一个政府助推小组。助推小组的成功催生了美国社会与行为科学团队，并对德国、荷兰、芬兰、新加坡和澳大利亚等国的决策者产生影响。[7]

《助推》还推动了 2014 年"全球首届公共政策行为洞察会议"的召开。[8]该大会现在每年举办一次。它的成功标志着学术界、决策者和媒体对《助推》持续关注。

1. 克里斯汀·焦尔斯等："法学和经济学的行为研究方法",《斯坦福法学评论》第50卷,1998年第5期,第1471—1550页。

2. 理查德·H. 泰勒和卡斯·R. 桑斯坦："自由主义的温和专制主义不是矛盾修辞法",《芝加哥大学法律评论》第70卷,2003年第4期。

3. 卡斯·R. 桑斯坦和理查德·H. 泰勒："自由主义的温和专制主义",第1202页。

4. 摩根·豪泽尔："丹尼尔·卡尼曼谈挑战经济假设",《彩衣傻瓜》,2013年6月29日,登录日期2015年9月4日,http://www.fool.com/investing/general/2013/06/29/challenging-assumptions-an-economist-considers-psy.aspx。

5. 摩根·豪泽尔："丹尼尔·卡尼曼谈挑战经济假设"。

6. 诺亚·史密斯："五位应该获得诺贝尔奖的经济学家",《彭博视野》,2014年12月9日,登录日期2015年9月4日,http://www.bloombergview.com/articles/2014–12–09/five-economists-who-deserve-nobels。

7. 行为洞察团队："行为洞察团队2013—2015年更新报告",登录日期2015年9月4日,http://behaviouralinsights.co.uk/wp-content/uploads/2015/07/BIT_Update-Report-Final–2013–2015.pdf。

8. 行为洞察团队:2014全球行为洞察会议,登录日期2015年9月30日,http://www.behaviouralinsights.co.uk/bx2015/behavioural-exchange–2014/。

第三部分：学术影响

9 最初反响

要点 ⌘━━

- 《助推》受到了两种主要批评：助推过于专制；助推只能在浅层次改变人们的行为。

- 泰勒和桑斯坦通过采访和发表的文章回应了他们的批评者。

- 泰勒和桑斯坦承认单凭助推无法解决重大的社会问题，但他们没有改变自己的基本立场。

批评

《助推》成为国际畅销书，被英国杂志《经济学人》[1]和《金融时报》[2]评为 2008 年最佳图书之一。然而，尽管《助推》取得了巨大成功，但它也受到了一些媒体和学者的批评。

《助推》受到的第一种批评是其过于专制的家长式作风。该书面世后不久，泰勒和美国经济学家理查德·波斯纳之间就发生了一场争论。争论的焦点是美国消费者金融保护局*，该机构为应对 2008 年金融危机而设立。受行为经济学研究的影响，消费者金融保护局的目标之一是通过使用"民众财务决策的实际数据"来保护消费者免受金融欺诈。[3]它要求金融机构向客户提供简单的"香草型"（指简单的、常见的）抵押贷款，抵押合同上所列的条款应简洁明了，在三分钟内即可读完。波斯纳在《华尔街日报》上严厉批评了这一提议。[4]他认为，"香草型"抵押贷款产品会增加金融机构提供其他类型抵押贷款的顾虑，这将减少市场竞争，令客户的境况更糟。

第二种批评是助推太过肤浅，无法应对重大的社会挑战。英国上议院（英国议会的两院之一）发布了一份关于行为改变的报告，详细阐述了这种批评。该报告的负责人朱莉娅·纽伯格男爵夫人*认为，严肃的行为改变需要的"不仅仅是助推……被纳入一揽子监管和财政措施中的干预似乎最有效"。[5] 该报告以肥胖问题为例，指出应该通过综合政策措施来解决受复杂的社会和环境因素影响的社会问题，而不仅仅是在个人层面进行助推。[6]

> "我们发现很关键的一点是，孤立使用某种非监管措施（包括'助推'）不太可能有效。有效的政策通常会使用一系列的干预措施。"
>
> —— 英国上议院科学技术特别委员会：《行为改变报告》

回应

自《助推》出版后，泰勒和桑斯坦通过大量的采访和文章回应了他们的批评者。

泰勒在美国公共广播公司《新闻一小时》栏目发表的一篇文章中驳斥了波斯纳对抵押贷款合同的指责，称其观点具有误导性。[7] 他认为，"香草型"金融产品合同格式不会限制消费者的选择，但会提供一个基准线，让消费者可以据此对其他产品做出判断。金融公司可以自由地为需要的人提供更复杂的产品。泰勒将其与标准租赁合同相比，后者为消费者提供了一个框架来识别房东是否提出了特别条款。这种参考框架有助于租客判断非标准条款是否符合他们的最佳利益。

桑斯坦在《卫报》发表的一篇文章中承认仅靠助推手段无法解

决最大的社会问题。他说："对于一些最严重的问题，比如暴力犯罪、贫困和气候变化，仅有助推是不够的……没有人否认规定和禁令的作用。"[8] 泰勒和桑斯坦他们自己从未说过，助推可以解决这类问题。这种批评指向政策制定者可能会更公平，他们忽视了税收和监管等传统政策工具，而倾向于采用助推手段，因为前者更难实施。

冲突与共识

面对早期受到的批评，泰勒和桑斯坦重申了《助推》的核心观点：真正的助推不限制选择的自由，对选择进行限制的政策制定者并没有遵循自由主义的温和专制主义理念。他们承认单靠助推并不能解决所有的社会问题，而他们自己也从未声称助推能解决一切问题。

在随后的辩论中，他们也受到了一些较难反驳的批评。《纽约书评》刊登的一篇《助推》书评批评道，助推往往利用的是决策过程中原本准备改善的缺陷。换句话说，助推通常针对快速、本能的直觉思维系统发挥作用，而不是缓慢、深思熟虑的理性思维系统。[9] 书评人说他自己更喜欢有意识地做出更明智的决策，而不是被悄悄地引向最佳决策。尽管桑斯坦对该作者的其他批评作出了回应，但没有对这一观点表态。[10]

---

1. "甄选"，《经济学人》，2008 年 12 月 4 日，登录日期 2015 年 9 月 4 日，http://www.economist.com/node/12719711。

2. "最佳商业书籍",《金融时报》, 2008 年, 登录日期 2015 年 9 月 4 日, http://ig.ft.com/sites/business-book-award/books/2008/longlist/nudge-by-richard-thaler-and-cass-sunstein。

3. 美国财政部:"金融规制改革执行综合报告:新基石", 2009 年 6 月 17 日, 登录日期 2015 年 9 月 4 日, http://www.treasury.gov/initiatives/wsr/Documents/executive_summary.pdf。

4. 理查德·波斯纳:"将金融消费者视为成年人",《华尔街日报》, 2009 年 7 月 22 日, 登录日期 2015 年 9 月 4 日, http://www.wsj.com/articles/SB10001424052970203946904574302213213148166。

5. 伊丽莎·戴:"茱莉亚·纽伯嘉:朝正确的方向助推无法运行大社会",《观察家报》, 2011 年 7 月 17 日, 登录日期 2015 年 9 月 4 日, http://www.theguardian.com/society/2011/jul/17/julia-neuberger-nudge-big-society。

6. 英国上议院科学技术特别委员会:"行为改变报告", 上议院文件第 179 卷, 2011 年, 登录日期 2015 年 9 月 4 日, http://www.publicatons.parliament.uk/pa/ld201012/ldselect/ldsctech/179/179.pdf。

7. 理查德·H.泰勒:"泰勒对波斯纳关于消费者保护的回应", 美国公共广播公司《新闻一小时》栏目, 2009 年 7 月 28 日, 登录日期 2015 年 9 月 4 日, http://www.pbs.org/newshour/making-sense/thaler-responds-to-posner-on-c/。

8. 卡斯·R.桑斯坦:"助推遭遇强烈反对——但它从来不是要解决所有问题",《卫报》, 2014 年 4 月 24 日, 登录日期 2015 年 9 月 4 日, http://www.theguardian.com/commentisfree/2014/apr/24/nudge-backlash-free-society-dignity-coercion。

9. 杰里米·沃尔德伦:"这都是为了你好",《纽约书评》, 2014 年 10 月 9 日, 登录日期 2015 年 9 月 4 日, http://www.nybooks.com/articles/archives/2014/oct/09/cass-sunstein-its-all-your-own-good/。

10. 卡斯·R.桑斯坦:"助推:善意的和恶意的",《纽约书评》, 2014 年 10 月 23 日, 登录日期 2015 年 9 月 4 日, http://nybooks.com/articles/archives/2014/oct/23/nudges-good-and-bad/。

10 后续争议

要点 🗝—

- "助推"一词现在被学术界和全球政策制定者广泛采用。

- 桑斯坦在其著作《为何助推?》中集中回应了针对《助推》的批评。

- 《助推》的成功导致许多干预被错误地描述为"行为经济学"。现在有使用更为宽泛的术语的倾向,比如"行为科学"和"行为洞察"。

应用与问题

泰勒和桑斯坦在《助推》一书中提出政府应该助推民众,这一观点被许多政策制定者和学者广泛接受。当前的辩论有两个值得注意的趋势。

第一个趋势是该书的观点持续受到批评。比利时哲学家卢克·柏文斯*指出助推是危险的,因为它们很微妙。[1]人们不会像注意到禁令或监管那样注意到助推,因此糟糕的助推可能不会像糟糕的监管那样引发相同的政治反应。另一种批评认为,《助推》指出了人类决策中一贯存在的缺陷——而决策者不可避免地也会受到这一缺陷的影响,那么,民众怎么能相信他们会做出明智的干预呢?[2]更进一步的批评是,由于助推的目的是阻止人们做出错误的选择,因此人们也就失去了从错误中吸取教训的机会。

桑斯坦在他的著作《为何助推?》[3]中回应了《助推》受到的一连串批评。美国心理学家巴里·施瓦茨*评价该书论证"细致而又精巧"。[4]

第二个趋势是大众媒体将行为改变与行为经济学几乎等同起来，这是《助推》的巨大成功带来的意外结果。丹尼尔·卡尼曼在《公共政策的行为基础》中对此进行了讨论。[5]他认为，许多认知与社会心理学研究在政策上的应用被错误地称为"行为经济学"。他补充说，泰勒自己"一直坚持对行为经济学的狭义定义，而且……更愿意看到'助推'被描述成行为科学的应用"。[6]

这看上去只是一个关于术语的浅层辩论，但它更深层的含义是，《助推》的成功使得心理学及社会科学的其他学科能够合法地参与政策制定。这是一个重大转变，因为一直以来经济学是唯一一个可以深度影响决策的学术领域。现在，人们有意识地使用"行为科学"等更宽泛的术语来描述行为改变干预。

> "助推的全部意义，英国以及现在其他一些国家创建行为洞察团队的全部意义，就是在政策设计上给非经济学家的普通民众以发言权。"
> ——理查德·H.泰勒，引自彼得·乌比尔："理查德·H.泰勒访谈录：'助推'的真正意义"，《福布斯》

思想流派

《助推》已然成为一个独特的思想流派。"助推"一词早已进入学者和决策者的语言中，世界上一些最有影响力的组织现在也在应用该书的理念。例如，全球金融机构世界银行[*]发布了"2015年世界发展报告：思维、社会与行为"，讨论如何在发展中国家的小微金融领域（一种为无法获得银行传统服务的个人和小群体提供的金融服务）采用助推方式。助推也被应用于艾滋病毒测试。[7]2013年，作为英国金融市场行为监管部门的英国金融行为监管局[*]发布了一份报告，描述了行为经济学和助推思想是如何影响其工作的。[8]行为经济学家皮特·伦恩[*]为经合组织[*]（全称为经济合作与发展组织，由一些主张通过市场经济体系促进民主与经济增长的国家组成）写了一个以行为经济学与监管政策（为应对金融危机或规划公共投资等目的而制定的政策）为主题的报告。[9]

《助推》已被引用5 000余次，在学术界影响深远。[10]更令人注目的是，引用该书的包括经济学、心理学、公共卫生、市场营销、社会学、医学、政治学、犯罪学和哲学等众多学科。

当代研究

英国的行为洞察团队可以说是当今传播《助推》思想最有影响力的组织。2010年，英国首相戴维·卡梅伦为了在保守党领导的新政府中实施该书的理念，成立了这个团队，也称"助推小组"。理查德·H. 泰勒是该团队的外部顾问，表明他的思想具有持久的影响力。

行为洞察团队设定的目标显然是受到了《助推》的启发。这些目标包括"帮助民众能够'为自己做出更好的选择'"，"提升公共服务成本效益，使之更便于民众使用"，以及"在政策中引入更实际的人类行为模式"。[11]然而，也有迹象表明，尽管该组织采纳了《助推》的理念，但它并不完全依附于此。其官网描述的研究方法并未使用"助推"一词，而其正式名称也使用了更为宽泛的术语"行为洞察"而非"行为经济学"。这反映了卡尼曼所讨论的趋势，即转向一种更广泛的行为干预研究方法，这种方法不受行为经济学的约束。

1. 卢克·柏文斯："助推伦理"，蒂尔·格鲁-亚诺夫和斯万·欧维·汉森编，《偏好变化：哲学、经济学和心理学的研究方法》，纽约：斯普林格出版社，2009年，第207—219页。

2. 简·施耐伦巴赫和克里斯蒂安·舒伯特："行为经济学：一项调查"，《欧洲政治经济学杂志》，2015年。

3. 卡斯·R.桑斯坦《为何助推？》，纽约：耶鲁大学出版社，2014年。

4. 巴里·施瓦茨，"为何不助推？——评卡斯·R.桑斯坦的《为何助推？》"，《心理学报告》，2014年4月17日，登录日期2015年9月4日，http://thepsychreport. com/essays-discussion/nudge-review-cass-sunsteins-why-nudge/。

5. 埃尔德·沙菲尔编：《公共政策的行为基础》，普林斯顿：普林斯顿大学出版社，2012年，第7页。

6. 埃尔德·沙菲尔编：《公共政策的行为基础》，第7页。

7. 世界银行："2015年世界发展报告：思维、社会与行为"，《世界银行集团旗舰报告》，2015年，登录日期2015年9月26日，www.worldbank.org/content/dam/ Worldbank/Publications/WDR/WDR%202015/WDR–2015–Full-Report.pdf。

8. 克里斯蒂·埃尔塔等："行为经济学在金融市场行为监管局的实践"，《金融行为管理局专题选刊》，2013年第1期，登录日期2015年9月4日，https://www.fca. org.uk/static/documents/occasional-papers/occasional-paper–1.pdf。

9. 皮特·伦恩：《监管政策与行为经济学》，巴黎：经合组织出版社，2014年。

10. 截至2015年9月26日谷歌学术记录了5 495条引用《助推》的文本，https:// scholar.google.com/scholar?cites=16854468477297806637&as_sdt=2005&sciodt=0,5&hl=en。

11. 行为洞察团队："我们是谁"，登录日期2015年9月4日，http://behaviouralinsights. co.uk/about-us/。

11 当代印迹

要点 🔑

- 《助推》是研究决策和公共政策的重要参考文献。
- 《助推》强调行为经济学和心理学对解读人类行为的作用,挑战了新古典经济学作为唯一能够影响政策制定的学科的主导地位。
- 尽管《助推》受到了批评,但是它的大部分理念被决策者、商人和学者所接受。

地位

《助推》出版不到 10 年,就已成为政界、学术界和商界研究人类决策和行为改变的重要参考文献。尽管《助推》受到了相当多的批评,但在一定程度上是因为,该书的巨大成功及其全球影响力使其成为一个非常明显的批评目标。桑斯坦在《为何助推?》一书中对这些批评做出了全面的回应,他认为选择架构和助推思想在未来将继续产生影响。

《助推》挑战了新古典经济学在政策制定中的传统主导地位。尽管泰勒和桑斯坦在行为经济学领域成就卓著,但他们都认为,总体而言,心理学研究应该在关于政策制定的辩论中发挥更大的作用。桑斯坦指出,美国总统有经济顾问委员会,而没有心理顾问委员会。[1]有鉴于此,两位作者都主张使用更宽泛的术语"行为科学"*。

"政治家必须……顺应民众的真实想法，而不是将自己的想法强加给他们，这样才能成功。如果将顺应人类的天性这一非常简单、非常保守的思想与所有行为经济学的研究成果结合起来……我认为我们能够真正提升社会福利和民众幸福，创建一个更强大的社会。"

——戴维·卡梅伦:"谈下一代的政府"，TED

互动

《助推》的成功及其对行为科学的促进极大地影响了英国的政策制定。在 2010 年到 2015 年之间，行为洞察团队（助推小组）发布了十多个报告，记录了他们在助推思想的影响下对劳动力市场、能源使用、反欺诈、税收、器官捐赠和慈善捐赠等方面进行的干预。他们取得的成功包括:

- 改写税务信函，加上诸如"你们镇上十位居民中有九位按时纳税"这样的语句，结果产生了数百万英镑的额外税收。[2]这种干预基于社会规范对行为影响的心理学研究。
- 设计一个成功帮助失业人员重新就业的项目。该项目要求求职者详细说明他们将如何找工作，而不是汇报他们承担过哪些工作。该项目还要求求职者写一篇自述文章，表明自己的长处。[3]
- 当人们在网上完成驾照更新手续时，顺便让他们填写人体器官捐赠意愿表，使得器官捐赠人数增多。[4]

行为洞察团队的成功大力宣传了由行为科学和科学方法论指导的决策理念。该组织的负责人大卫·哈尔彭*认为他们的做法是未来的发展方向。他说:"我想我们会在 10 年或 20 年后回头看，然后说，'你以为我们当时没这样做吗？'"[5]

持续争议

《助推》在学术界引起了不同的反响。英国健康心理学家苏珊·米基*是其中一位著名的批评者，她认为助推理念在改变不健康行为方面具有局限性。她强调，吸烟和肥胖等行为通常受社区和人群状况的影响，而不仅仅取决于个人因素。例如，如果一个胖子处于饮食不健康的生活环境中，鼓励他少喝苏打水可能不会对减肥产生效果。米基提出了"行为改变轮"理论，它为设计干预措施提供了更为详细的框架，会考虑多层次因素。[6]

主流经济学对《助推》的反应又是如何呢？该书根植于行为经济学领域，而行为经济学正是在对新古典经济学中人类行为假设的批判中发展起来的。卡尼曼曾说过："这些假设受到了挑战，但经济学仍然一如既往。"[7]这听起来可能过于悲观。行为经济学家科林·凯莫勒和乔治·罗文斯坦认为行为经济学不是一场意图取代新古典经济学的革命；相反，其思想将被新古典主义经济学吸收。[8]它最有价值的贡献在于提出了"一刀切"的理性人模型——人们依据所拥有的信息理性地做出经济决策——并非总是解读人类行为的合适工具。在泰勒看来，"心理学没有统一的理论……行为经济学的理论也会多元化。"[9]由于《助推》出版尚不足 10 年，它对主流经济学的长期影响仍有待观察。

---

1. 卡斯·R. 桑斯坦："心理顾问委员会"，《心理学年鉴》，登录日期 2015 年 9

月 4 日，http://dash.harvard.edu/bitstream/handle/1/13031653/annualreview9_15.pdf? sequence=1。

2. 行为洞察团队："运用行为经济学智慧减少欺诈、错误和债务"，2012 年 2 月，登录日期 2015 年 9 月 4 日，https://www.gov.uk/government/uploads/system/uploads/attachment_data/file/60539/BIT_FraudErrorDebt_accessible.pdf。

3. 卡特琳·本霍尔德："英国人的助推部"，《纽约时报》，2013 年 12 月 7 日，登录日期 2015 年 9 月 4 日，http://www.nytimes.com/2013/12/08/business/international/britains-ministry-of-nudges.html?_r=0。

4. 行为洞察团队："运用行为经济学智慧增加慈善捐赠"，登录日期 2015 年 9 月 4 日，https://gov.uk/government/uploads/system/uploads/attachment_data/file/203286/BIT_Charitable_Giving_Paper.pdf。

5. 卡特琳·本霍尔德："英国人的助推部"。

6. 苏珊·米基等："行为改变轮：描述和设计行为改变干预的新方法"，《实施科学》2011 年第 6 卷，第 42 篇。

7. 摩根·豪泽尔："尼尔·卡尼曼谈挑战经济假设"，《彩衣傻瓜》，2013 年 9 月 29 日，登录日期 2015 年 9 月 4 日，http://www.fool.com/investing/general/2013/06/29/challenging-assumptions-an-economist-considers-psy.aspx。

8. 科林·凯莫勒和乔治·罗文斯坦："行为经济学：过去、现在和未来"，科林·凯莫勒等编，《行为经济学研究进展》，普林斯顿：普利斯顿大学出版社，2003 年。

9. 理查德·H. 泰勒："何时会有一个统一的'行为'经济理论？"，选自"你的领域里害怕被问到的问题是什么？"，《边缘》，2014 年 3 月 28 日，登录日期 2015 年 9 月 4 日，http://edge.org/conversation/whats-the-question-about-your-field-that-you-dread-being-asked#25056。

12 未来展望

要点 🔑

- 《助推》可能会继续激发全球学术界和政策制定者的兴趣。
- 《助推》最重要的长期影响可能是促进国家治理规范的科学化。
- 《助推》推动行为经济学走向全球，提倡以证据为基础的决策方式，具有开创性意义。

潜力

《助推》将会继续促进一系列学科的学术研究。该书是大学行为经济学课程的标准参考书，被成千上万的论文和报告引用。在政治决策领域，该书的思想吸引了世界银行、[1]经合组织、[2]英国上议院，[3]以及美国、英国、德国、荷兰、芬兰、新加坡和澳大利亚等各国政府的关注。[4]助推思想极大地影响了税收、金融、移民、慈善捐赠、能源效率和可持续性、反犯罪和欺诈、失业、教育、网络安全以及国际发展等各个领域。[5]

> "选择架构和助推将在其他领域内引发对改善人类生活的创造性思考，这是我们的主要愿望之一。"
> ——理查德·H.泰勒和卡斯·R.桑斯坦：
> 《助推：如何做出有关健康、财富和幸福的更优决策》

未来方向

从长期来看，《助推》最重要的贡献可能是促进形成了两条基于科学研究的政策制定准则。

第一条准则是决策者应该利用最可靠的科研成果来设计他们的干预措施。这似乎意味着不能仅仅依靠《助推》提出的想法，因为此类干预受限于行为经济学原理和自由主义的温和专制主义，相对狭窄。这个趋势已经显现。英国和美国助推小组的正式名称中都没有使用"助推"或"行为经济学"这两个词汇。具体名称分别为英国行为洞察团队与美国社会与行为科学团队。"行为洞察力"和"社会与行为科学"的意义更为宽泛。这两个名称表明其组织不仅仅使用《助推》提出的理论和干预工具，也为其采用其他学科的科学证据和其他干预工具留出了自由空间。

第二条准则是决策者应该使用诸如随机对照试验*之类的科学方法长期测试干预的有效性。随机对照试验是社会科学用来评价干预有效性的黄金标准。这种趋势也已显现。2012年，英国助推小组和一些学者联合发表了题为《测试、学习、适应：用随机对照试验制定公共政策》的报告，认为英国政策制定者应该使用随机对照试验来测试干预措施的有效性。[6]美国奥巴马政府也赞同采用随机对照试验方法，称政府必须通过"严格的证据和评估来确保纳税人的资金进行了明智的投资"。[7]泰勒也谈到了在决策过程中使用随机对照试验的必要性。他说："没有证据，就无法做出基于事实、依据充分的决策。"[8]

这条准则由英国行为洞察团队和美国社会与行为科学团队直接推动后形成，两者的年度报告中均详细地记录了他们实施干预行为的具体方式及其有效性评估情况。经济学家贾斯汀·沃尔弗斯在《纽约时报》的一篇评论文章中对这个趋势表达了赞同："最重要的……不在于知道如何做得更好，而在于测试什么是有效的。坚持不懈地试验，保留有效的，摒弃无效的。按照这个方法，就会产生一个……透明、人性化和极为高效的政府。"[9]

虽然《助推》并没有直接提出这两个准则，但它在全球范围内的成功，以及强调决策要基于证据，都突显了这些准则的重要性。

小结

《助推》提出了一个很有说服力的观点，认为政府可以在不限制民众选择自由的情况下改善他们的生活。它利用行为经济学和心理学的证据来支持这一观点，并就政策制定者如何应用助推思想提出了具体的、明智的建议。它在全球的影响力代表着行为经济学及其人类决策理论的重大成功。

行为经济学的兴起映射出理查德·H.泰勒在主流经济学家中不断高涨的声誉。用哈佛大学经济学教授大卫·莱布森的话来说，"在20世纪80年代的大部分时间里，（泰勒）一直被视为怪人……在长达十年的时间里他虽然屡遭质疑但始终坚持自己的立场，这需要莫大的勇气。泰勒一直在战斗，最终几乎得到了所有人的认可。"[10] 2015年，泰勒出任美国经济学协会主席，这表明他那些曾经被认为激进的观点已为主流经济学所接受。

---

1. 世界银行："2015年世界发展报告：思维、社会与行为"，世界银行集团旗舰报告，2015年，登录日期2015年9月26日，http://www.worldbank.org/content/dam/Worldbank/Publications/WDR/WDR%202015/WDR–2015-Full-Report.pdf。

2. 皮特·伦恩:《监管政策与行为经济学》,巴黎:经合组织出版社,2014 年。

3. 英国上议院科学技术特别委员会:"行为改变报告",《上议院文件》第 179 卷,2011 年,登录日期 2015 年 9 月 4 日,http://www.publicatons.parliament.uk/pa/ld201012/ldselect/ldsctech/179/179.pdf。

4. 行为洞察团队"行为洞察团队 2013—2015 年更新报告",登录日期 2015 年 9 月 4 日,http://www.behaviouralinsights.co.uk/wp-content/uploads/2015/07/BIT_Update-Report-Final–2013-2015.pdf。

5. 行为洞察团队:"行为洞察团队 2013—2015 年更新报告"。

6. 劳拉·海恩斯等:"测试、学习、适应:用随机对照试验制定公共政策",英国内阁办公室,2012 年 6 月,登录日期 2015 年 9 月 4 日,https://www.gov.uk/government/uploads/system/uploads/attachment_data/file/62529/TLA–1906126.pdf。

7. 汤姆·卡利尔:"有效的资助:低成本随机对照试验的重要性",白宫博客,2014 年 7 月 9 日,登录日期 2015 年 9 月 4 日,https://www.whitehouse.gov/blog/2014/07/09/funding-what-works-importance-low-cost-randomizd-controlled-trials。

8. 理查德·H.泰勒:"制定规则之前要观察行为",《纽约时报》,2012 年 7 月 7 日,登录日期 2015 年 9 月 4 日,http://www.nytimes.com/2012/07/08/business/behavioral-science-can-help-guide-policy-economic-view.html。

9. 贾斯丁·沃尔弗斯:"渐进成为更好的政府",《纽约时报》,2015 年 9 月 25 日,登录日期 2015 年 9 月 30 日,http://www.nytimes.com/2015/09/27/upshot/a-better-government-one-tweak-at-a-time.html?rref=upshot&_r=0。

10. 格里高利·卡普:"简介:理查德·H.泰勒,芝加哥大学布斯商学院教授",《芝加哥论坛报》,2012 年 4 月 30 日,登录日期 2015 年 9 月 4 日,http://articles.chicagotribune.com/2012–04–30/business/ct-biz–0430-executive-profile-thaler-20120430_1_economics-daniel-kahneman-cost-fallacy。

术语表

1. **"反常现象"**：理查德·H. 泰勒于 20 世纪 80 年代和 90 年代在《经济展望杂志》上开设的颇具影响力的专栏，是向主流经济学者介绍行为经济学研究的平台。

2. **直觉思维系统和理性思维系统**：心理学和神经科学认为人的大脑中存在两套截然不同的思维系统，分别是直觉思维系统和理性思维系统。在直觉思维系统中人依靠直觉和本能迅速做出判断和决策，而在理性思维系统中人经过思考和权衡做出判断和决策。

3. **可得性启发**：一种认知经验法则，指人们把容易回忆起来的经验和信息作为判断依据。

4. **行为经济学**：经济学的一个分支学科，该学科将心理学的研究整合到经济决策模型之中。

5. **行为科学**：一门综合行为经济学、心理学和其他学科的理论和方法，研究人的行为的学科。

6. **行为洞察团队**：英国前首相戴维·卡梅伦于 2010 年设立的重要组织，旨在政府内部推行助推理念。

7. **芝加哥学派**：与芝加哥大学经济学系相关联的新古典主义经济学流派。

8. **选择架构**：指人们做决策时所处的环境。

9. **认知偏差**：是一种认知世界的方式，这种方式会造成系统性偏差，使人偏离理性的、正确的判断。

10. **保守党**：英国右翼政党派别，成立于 1834 年。

11. **宪法性法律**：指从国家宪法派生出来的一系列法律。

12. **消费者金融保护局**：美国政府机构，成立于 2011 年，负责保护金融消费者的权益。

13. **民主党**：美国的两大主要政党之一。成立于 1828 年，是中左翼政党。

14. **《计量经济学》**：经济学领域最重要的期刊之一，创刊于 1933 年。

15. **经济人与社会人**：泰勒和桑斯坦将经济模型中完美的理性决策者称为"经济人"，而将现实世界中的普通决策者称为"社会人"。

16. **金融行为监管局**：英国金融服务行业的监管机构。

17. **启发**：指决策过程中使用的经验法则。

18. **《经济展望杂志》**：经济学综合期刊，创刊于 1987 年。

19. **司法极简主义**：一种主张对美国宪法性法律进行渐近式解读的法律哲学，支持法院在司法实践中，只局限于解决个案问题，而无须决定其他事项。

20. **工党**：英国中左翼政党。

21. **自由主义**：一种强调个体自由和选择自由的政治哲学。

22. **自由主义的温和专制主义**：《助推》一书中提出的理念。泰勒和桑斯坦主张引导人们做出最佳决策的同时又不限制人们选择的自由，即"温和的专制主义"。

23. **损失厌恶**：指人面对相同数量的收益和损失时，更愿意避免损失的倾向。

24. **新古典主义经济学**：第二次世界大战后发展起来的主流经济学思潮。新古典主义经济学以理性人假设为基本前提，在这个行为模型下，人们具有完备的信息，总是理性地做出最优选择。

25. **助推**：指在选择体系中采用某些措施，以可预见的方式去改变人们的行为。同时，这些措施不需要付出什么成本很容易就能避免。

26. **助推小组**：行为洞察团队的非正式名称。

27. **奥巴马政府**：贝拉克·奥巴马美国总统大选获胜后组建的美国政

府，任期为 2009 年 1 月至 2017 年 1 月。

28. **经合组织**：即经济合作与发展组织，是一个由多国组成的政府间组织，主张通过市场经济系统促进民主与经济增长。

29. **温和专制主义**：指个人或组织以代表他人利益为理由限制被代表人的选择自由的行为。

30. **"前景理论"**：丹尼尔·卡尼曼与阿莫斯·特沃斯基合著的一篇关于行为经济学的开创性论文，于 1979 年发表在《计量经济学》期刊上。

31. **随机对照试验**：社会科学用来评价干预效果的一种方法，被认为是黄金标准。

32. **理性人**：指根据理性选择理论假说从事经济活动的人。

33. **理性选择理论**：新古典主义经济学为了研究人的经济行为与社会行为而采用的主要理论和方法。

34. **"保守主义人士也能接受的规制"**：行为经济学家科林·凯莫勒与同事于 2003 年合著发表的一篇论文。该论文提出的"不对称家长式作风"概念与《助推》一书中提出的"自由主义的温和专制主义"概念相似。

35. **共和党**：美国的两大主要政党之一。成立于 1854 年，右翼政党。

36. **《科学》**：世界最权威的科学学术期刊之一，创刊于 1880 年。

37. **社会与行为科学团队**：美国总统贝拉克·奥巴马于 2015 年发布行政命令正式设立的一个机构，旨在推进行为科学在联邦政府内的应用。

38. **《道德情操论》**：苏格兰哲学家亚当·斯密创作的伦理学著作，1759 年出版，被认为是行为经济学的理论基石。

39. **第三条道路**：20 世纪许多政治人士对一种政治立场的表述。"第三条道路"主张同时采纳左翼政党与右翼政党的部分政策，试图调和这两大政治意识形态的差异。泰勒与桑斯坦认为他们提出的"自由主义的温和专制主义"是"真正的第三条道路"。

40. **2008 年金融危机**：被认为是继 20 世纪 30 年代经济大萧条后发达国家遭遇的最严重的经济衰退。

41. **世界银行**：一个为消除全球贫困而设立的国际性组织，通过为发展中国家提供贷款的方式支持其发展基础设施。

42. **第二次世界大战**：指 1939 年至 1945 年间发生的全球规模的战争。战争双方分别为法西斯轴心国（包括德国、意大利和日本）和反法西斯同盟国（包括英国、苏联、美国和其他国家）。第二次世界大战是 20 世纪标志性事件之一，对世界格局产生了巨大的影响。

人名表

1. 约翰·贝西尔斯，哈佛商学院商业管理教授，研究行为经济学在个体决策和市场表现中的应用。

2. 卢克·柏文斯（1961年生），比利时哲学家，伦敦政治经济学院教授，研究助推涉及的伦理问题。

3. 科林·凯莫勒（1959年生），美国行为经济学家，加州理工学院行为金融学和经济学教授。他与同事一同提出了"不对称家长式作风"的概念，与《助推》中提出的"自由主义的温和专制主义"相似。

4. 戴维·卡梅伦（1966年生），英国前首相，任期为2010年至2016年。

5. 沃纳·德·邦特，比利时经济学家，曾与理查德·H.泰勒合作研究行为金融学。

6. 米尔顿·弗里德曼（1912—2006），芝加哥经济学派代表人物，20世纪最具影响力的经济学家之一，1976年获诺贝尔经济学奖。

7. 大卫·哈尔彭，英国心理学家，英国行为洞察团队即助推小组负责人。

8. 克里斯汀·焦尔斯（1967年生），美国法学家，耶鲁大学法学院教授，研究行为经济学在法律领域的应用。

9. 丹尼尔·卡尼曼（1934年生），以色列心理学家，与阿莫斯·特沃斯基合作在决策研究方面做出卓越贡献，于2002年获诺贝尔经济学奖。现为普林斯顿大学心理学及公共事务专业荣誉教授。

10. 大卫·莱布森（1966年生），美国行为经济学家，哈佛大学经济学教授。他著有数篇有影响力的论文，研究有限度的自我控制对经济行为的影响。

11. 乔治·罗文斯坦（1955年生），美国行为经济学家，卡耐基梅隆大学经济学和心理学教授。他与科林·凯莫勒合著介绍行为经济学发展史。

12. **皮特·伦恩**，爱尔兰经济学家，研究行为经济学在监管与公共政策领域的应用。

13. **布里吉特·马德里安**，哈佛大学肯尼迪政治学院公共政策教授。2000年与丹尼斯·谢伊合作研究养老金登记项目中默认设置的重要性。

14. **苏珊·米基**（1955年生），英国伦敦大学健康心理学教授。她批评助推理论在健康干预方面的局限性，提出了"行为改变轮"框架。

15. **埃德·米利班德**（1969年生），英国政治家，曾于2010至2015年任英国工党领袖。

16. **朱莉娅·纽伯格男爵夫人**（1950年生），英国上议院议员。她是2001年英国上议院关于行为改变报告的负责人，该报告研究了助推的应用效果。

17. **贝拉克·奥巴马**（1961年生），美国第44位总统，任期为2009年至2017年。

18. **乔治·奥斯本**（1971年生），英国前首席国务大臣和财政大臣。

19. **理查德·波斯纳**（1939年生），美国法学学者和经济学家，著名的行为经济学评论家。

20. **巴里·施瓦茨**（1946年生），美国心理学家，研究决策心理。

21. **丹尼斯·谢伊**，2000年时任美国最大的健康保障公司联合健康集团副总裁，与布里吉特·马德里安共同研究养老金登记制度。

22. **赫伯特·西蒙**（1916—2001），美国心理学家，于1978年获得诺贝尔经济学奖。他提出了"有限理性"概念，并将其作为解读人类决策行为的基础。

23. **亚当·斯密**（1723—1790），苏格兰哲学家，因著有《国富论》和《道德情操论》而被尊为"现代经济学之父"。

24. **阿莫斯·特沃斯基**（1937—1996），以色列心理学家，因与丹尼尔·卡尼曼共同研究人类决策而著名。

WAYS IN TO THE TEXT

- The economist Richard H. Thaler and legal scholar Cass R. Sunstein are prominent American academics who worked together at the University of Chicago in the 1990s and the 2000s.

- In *Nudge: Improving Decisions about Health, Wealth, and Happiness*, Thaler and Sunstein introduced "libertarian paternalism,"* "choice architecture,"* and "nudging"* as tools for governments to help people make better decisions while respecting their freedom of choice.

- *Nudge* has influenced policy-making in the United Kingdom, United States, and several other countries. It is one of the most influential public policy books in recent years.

Who Are Richard H. Thaler and Cass R. Sunstein?

Richard H. Thaler, coauthor of *Nudge: Improving Decisions about Health, Wealth, and Happiness* (2008), was born in 1945. He completed his PhD in Economics at the University of Rochester in 1974 and has worked at the University of Chicago since 1995. Early in his career, Thaler was introduced to the work of the Israeli psychologists Daniel Kahneman* and Amos Tversky,* who would become important influences. Thaler became professor of behavioral science and economics at the Chicago Booth School of Business and established himself as a founding figure in the field of behavioral economics* (a subdiscipline of the field of economics which draws on findings from the discipline of psychology to formulate models of economic decision-making). Many academics consider Thaler a likely future winner of the Nobel Prize in

Economics.[1]

Cass R. Sunstein was born in 1954 and graduated from Harvard Law School in 1978. He worked at the University of Chicago from 1981 to 2008. During that time he wrote several articles applying behavioral economics to law and in total has published over 500 articles on a diverse set of topics. From 2009 to 2012 he served in the Obama Administration.* Currently the Robert Walmsley University Professor at Harvard, Sunstein is one of the most cited legal scholars in the world today.

In the 1990s, Thaler and Sunstein began to write *Nudge* at the University of Chicago, considered by many academics to be the home of the Chicago school*—an approach to economic theory known as neoclassical economics.* According to neoclassical economic theory, people make rational economic decisions on the basis of complete information. While, for the most part, *Nudge* strongly disagrees with this assumption, Thaler and Sunstein did not reject all the ideas of the Chicago school; their work builds on the influential Chicago economist Milton Friedman's* idea that people should be "free to choose."[2]

What Does *Nudge* Say?

In *Nudge*, Thaler and Sunstein argue that governments can help people make better decisions while respecting their freedom of choice.

Governments can do this by creating better "choice architecture." A choice architect designs the environment in which people make decisions. A simple example is a cafeteria manager who encourages healthy eating by placing vegetables first in a line of food options. Changing the choice architecture like this to encourage a certain behavior is what Thaler and Sunstein call a "nudge." Other examples of a nudge might be a driver's satellite navigation system, a sign that encourages people to take the stairs instead of the elevator, or government nutritional guidelines. These things encourage people to behave in a certain way, but do not force them to do so.

Thaler and Sunstein argue that governments should nudge people to make better decisions. However, people themselves must judge these decisions as "better," not the government. Thaler and Sunstein call their philosophy "libertarian paternalism."

This may seem a contradiction: libertarianism* is a political philosophy that emphasizes individual freedom and opposes government intervention, while paternalism* means to act on a person's behalf for what is deemed to be their own good. But Thaler and Sunstein reconcile this contradiction through a subtle argument. They say that interventions are permissible provided they do not restrict freedom of choice, giving the example of a firm that wants its workers to save more.[3] The firm nudges them to do so by enrolling them in a pension plan, but if the employees wish to opt out, they can do so. The general tendency of people to stick with a default option causes the savings rate to increase. This nudge also preserves freedom of choice because employees can choose not to use the plan.

Thaler and Sunstein argue that nudges can have significant and predictable effects, rejecting the assumptions underlying the main economic theories of human behavior. Many economists assume a model of behavior in which people are perfectly informed, have infinite cognitive ability, and unlimited self-control. Nudges cannot affect these "rational actors."* *Nudge* argues that real people have natural limitations in knowledge, cognitive ability, and self-control. Cognitive biases* (ways of interpreting the world that lead people away from rational judgments and behavior) and social pressures influence their decisions. Nudges can affect them.

Thaler and Sunstein call these groups "Econs"* (ideal decision-makers in economic models) and "Humans" (people who make decisions in the real world), and maintain that nudges can help Humans make better decisions. To support their argument, they cite decades of research in psychology and behavioral economics, showing how psychological factors can cause people to make poor decisions.

Thaler and Sunstein positioned their policies as a "real third way"*4 for American politics. They hoped nudging could appeal both to Democrats,* traditionally supportive of government intervention, and Republicans,* traditionally opposed to it.

Why Does *Nudge* Matter?

Nudge is one of the most influential books on public policy published in recent years. Its ideas are relevant to public policy, academic research, and private business. It has made its mark in all three fields.

In the United Kingdom, the right-wing Conservative party* embraced the book's ideas almost immediately after publication.

In 2010, Prime Minister David Cameron* created the world's first governmental "Nudge Unit"* (officially called the Behavioural Insights Team*). That group's success inspired the creation of the American Social and Behavioral Sciences Team* in 2015. *Nudge* has also influenced civil servants in Germany, the Netherlands, Finland, Singapore, and Australia.[5]

Nudge has stimulated a great deal of interest in the academic world. It has received over 5,000 citations from economics, psychology, public health, marketing, sociology, medicine, political science, criminology, philosophy, and other disciplines.[6] Many of these disciplines have adapted the book's ideas to new contexts and problems.

The ideas of *Nudge* also apply to the business world. A 2008 article in the *Harvard Business Review* describes how businesses can nudge their customers to buy their products.[7] A 2014 article in *Forbes* describes the way behavioral economics has affected the advertising industry as a whole.[8] Google has applied the book's ideas by using nudges in their company cafeteria.[9]

Thaler and Sunstein have continued to promote *Nudge* since its publication. Thaler has advised the Nudge Unit on tax collection and energy efficiency.[10] Sunstein applied the book's ideas as administrator of the Office of Information and Regulatory Affairs from 2009 to 2012. Both have engaged with the book's critics through interviews, articles, and books.

Nudge remains essential reading for anyone interested in the science of behavior change.

1. Noah Smith, "Five Economists Who Deserve Nobels," *Bloomberg View*, December 9, 2014, accessed September 4, 2015, http://www.bloombergview.com/articles/2014–12–09/five-economists-who-deserve-nobels.

2. Richard H. Thaler and Cass R. Sunstein, *Nudge: Improving Decisions about Health, Wealth, and Happiness* (New York: Yale University Press, 2008), 5.

3. Thaler and Sunstein, *Nudge*, 109.

4. Thaler and Sunstein, *Nudge*, 252.

5. Behavioural Insights Team, "The Behavioural Insights Team Update Report 2013–2015," accessed September 4, 2015, http://www.behaviouralinsights.co.uk/wp-content/uploads/2015/07/BIT_Update-Report-Final–2013–2015.pdf.

6. Google Scholar records 5,495 texts which have cited *Nudge* as of September 26, 2015: https://scholar.google. com/scholar?cites=16854468477297806637&as_ sdt=2005&sciodt=0,5&hl=en.

7. Daniel G. Goldstein et al., "Nudge Your Customers toward Better Choices," *Harvard Business Review*, December 2008, accessed September 4, 2015, https://hbr.org/2008/12/nudge-your-customers-toward-better-choices.

8. John Orwid, "Behavioral Economics Gives the Advertising Industry a Nudge in the Right Direction," *Forbes*, February 5, 2014, accessed September 26, 2015, http://www.forbes.com/sites/johnowrid/2014/02/05/behavioural-economics-gives-the-advertising-industry-a-nudge-in-the-right-direction/.

9. Cliff Kuang, "In the Cafeteria, Google Gets Healthy," *Fast Company Magazine*, March 19, 2012, accessed September 4, 2015, http://www. fastcompany.com/1822516/cafeteria-google-gets-healthy.

10. Douglas Clement, "Interview with Richard H. Thaler," *The Region Magazine*, October 3, 2013, accessed September 4, 2015, https://www. minneapolisfed.org/publications/the-region/interview-with-richard-thaler.

SECTION 1
INFLUENCES

THE AUTHORS AND THE HISTORICAL CONTEXT

KEY POINTS

* *Nudge* is one of the most significant books on public policy published in recent years.

* Its authors were influenced by studies in psychology about human decision-making, particularly work by the Israeli psychologists Daniel Kahneman* and Amos Tversky.*

* In *Nudge*, Thaler and Sunstein use theories from behavioral economics* to argue that governments should help their citizens to make better decisions while respecting their freedom of choice.

Why Read This Text?

In 2008, Richard H. Thaler, professor of behavioral science and economics at the University of Chicago, and Cass R. Sunstein, then professor of jurisprudence at the University of Chicago, published *Nudge: Improving Decisions about Health, Wealth, and Happiness.*

Their main argument in *Nudge* is that governments can help people make better decisions while respecting their freedom of choice. This can be achieved by organizing the environment in which people make decisions—what Thaler and Sunstein call choice architecture*—for example, the cafeteria that promotes healthy eating by putting fruits first and desserts last. Other examples might be a firm that automatically enrolls its employees into a retirement savings program while allowing them to opt out, or a website that recommends products based on your past purchases. These examples all encourage certain behaviors without banning any options or forcing any particular choice. Thaler and Sunstein call these kinds of interventions "nudges."*

In the seven years since its publication, *Nudge* has received over 5,000 citations and influenced a diverse set of academic disciplines.[1] It has directly influenced policy-making at the highest levels of government in the United Kingdom and United States. It has influenced firms in marketing, consulting, management, and many other industries. *Nudge* remains essential reading for anyone interested in the science of decision-making and behavior change.

> *"Yes, there is such a thing as common sense ... That's this reader's reaction to Richard H. Thaler and Cass R. Sunstein's 'Nudge,' an engaging and insightful tour through the evidence that most human beings don't make decisions [as they do] in elementary economics textbooks, along with a rich array of suggestions for enabling many of us to make better choices, both for ourselves and for society."*
>
> —— Benjamin M. Friedman, "Guiding Forces,"
> *New York Times*

Authors' Lives

Richard H. Thaler received his PhD in economics in 1974. Although he was taught economic theories that assumed perfectly rational models of human decision-making, early in his career Thaler was influenced by the Israeli psychologists Daniel

Kahneman and Amos Tversky, whose work contradicted these assumptions about human rationality. Thaler later integrated their insights (and other work from psychology) into economics to become a founding figure in the new field of behavioral economics. *Nudge* was based on theories from this field.

Cass R. Sunstein graduated with a JD from Harvard Law School in 1975. He has written prolifically throughout his career, including several influential texts applying the ideas of behavioral economics to law. Sunstein is also a noted proponent of judicial minimalism,* a legal philosophy that argues for small, case-specific interpretations of constitutional law* (those laws enshrined in a country's constitution). This philosophy may be indicative of Sunstein's preference for the incremental, "soft," interventions discussed in *Nudge*.

Thaler and Sunstein wrote *Nudge* during their shared tenure at the University of Chicago during the 1990s and 2000s. Ironically, the Chicago school* is considered the home of traditional neoclassical economics,* which *Nudge* rebelled against—particularly its assumption that people make economic decisions with perfect rationality. The authors did not, however, entirely reject the ideas of the Chicago school: the concept of nudging builds on the Chicago economist Milton Friedman's* idea that people should be "free to choose."[2]

Authors' Background

In the opening chapters of *Nudge*, Thaler and Sunstein introduce the historical context for their arguments by presenting two opposing schools of thought on human decision-making.

The first is the rational actor* model used in neoclassical economics. This has served as the bedrock of mainstream economic thinking since the post-World War II* era (the period from 1946). It proposes an abstract model of human behavior in which people behave completely rationally.

The second school of thought follows theories of behavioral economics. These ideas evolved in reaction to the rational actor model, which behavioral economists considered unrealistic. Behavioral economists aim to produce more realistic models of human decision-making based on psychological research into how people behave in the real world. This field was particularly influenced by work on flaws in human decision-making by Daniel Kahneman and Amos Tversky.

Nudge was published during the 2008 global financial crisis.* During that time, and in subsequent years, neoclassical economics was criticized by media figures[3] and academics[4] for its failure to foresee the crisis. In 2010, the Chicago-school economist Richard Posner* acknowledged that the crisis had created a "challenge to the economics profession as a whole, but to Chicago most of all."[5] The crisis led to an increased interest in behavioral economics as an alternative school of thought for understanding economic behavior.[6] In 2010, the future British prime minister, David Cameron, noted another consequence of the crisis, saying "the most important fact to bear in mind in British politics or American politics is: we have run out of money."[7] In that same talk, Cameron approvingly cited the ideas of behavioral economics as a way of achieving "a stronger society without necessarily having to spend a whole lot more money."[8] Both these factors helped create a more receptive atmosphere for the ideas of behavioral economics described in *Nudge*, particularly in the UK.

1. Google Scholar records 5,495 texts which have cited *Nudge* as of September 26, 2015: https://scholar. google. com/scholar?cites=16854468477297806637&as_ sdt=2005&sciodt=0,5&hl=en.

2. Richard H. Thaler and Cass R. Sunstein, *Nudge: Improving Decisions about Health, Wealth, and Happiness* (New York: Yale University Press, 2008), 5.

3. FT View, "Economics Needs to Reflect a Post-Crisis World," *Financial Times*, September 25, 2014, accessed October 15, 2015, http://www.ft.com/cms/s/0/f9f65e88–44a3–11e4–ab0c–00144feabdc0. html#axzz3ojq0z1zz.

4. Paul Krugman, "How Did Economists Get It So Wrong?," *New York Times*, September 6, 2009, accessed September 26, 2015, http://www.econ.ucdavis.edu/faculty/kdsalyer/LECTURES/Ecn200e/ krugman_macro.pdf.

5. John Cassidy, "After the Blowup," *New Yorker*, January 11, 2010, accessed September 26, 2015, http://www.newyorker.com/magazine/2010/01/11/after-the-blowup.

6. "Behavioural Finance to the Rescue?" *Economist*, August 18, 2009, accessed September 26, 2015, http://www.economist.com/blogs/freeexchange/2009/08/behavioural_finance_to_the_res.

7. David Cameron, "The Next Age of Government," *TED*, February 2010, accessed September 4, 2015, http://www.ted.com/talks/david_ cameron?language=en.

8. Cameron, "Next Age of Government."

MODULE 2
ACADEMIC CONTEXT

KEY POINTS

* The economic school of neoclassical economics* assumes a model of human decision-making in which people are perfectly rational.

* Thaler's insight, drawn from the work of the psychologists Kahneman* and Tversky,* was that sometimes people could consistently behave "irrationally" in a predictable way.

* Thaler integrated this insight into conventional economic thinking to become a founding figure in the field of behavioral economics.*

The Work in Its Context

Richard H. Thaler and Cass R. Sunstein's *Nudge: Improving Decisions about Health, Wealth, and Happiness* is grounded in the theories of behavioral economics. This discipline integrates research from psychology into economics with the goal of producing more realistic models of human decision-making. In their review of the history of behavioral economics, the American behavioral economists Colin Camerer* and George Loewenstein* identify Adam Smith's* 1759 book *The Theory of Moral Sentiments* as the foundational text of the discipline for its insights into the psychological principles of individual behavior.[1]

Camerer and Loewenstein date the modern discipline of behavioral economics as beginning in the second half of the twentieth century out of opposition to the use of rational choice theory* in neoclassical economics. That theory describes a simplified model of human decision-making in which people behave as "rational actors,"* with complete information about the choices available to them, perfect cognitive ability, and infinite self-control. In *Nudge*, Thaler and Sunstein criticize these assumptions as unrealistic. They describe rational actors as people who "can think like Albert Einstein, store as much memory as IBM's [supercomputer] Big Blue, and exercise the willpower of [the Indian political leader] Mahatma Gandhi."[2]

> "My greatest inspiration came from Kahneman and Tversky."
> ──Richard H. Thaler, quoted in Elina Halonen,
> "Research Heroes: Richard H. Thaler," *InDecision Blog*

Overview of the Field

While economists have long been aware of the criticisms of the rational choice theory,[3] one benefit was that it allowed them to make clear predictions about economic behavior. Many of these predictions were borne out by empirical evidence (evidence verifiable by observation) such as people buying less of a product when the price goes up, and working more when wages rise, suggesting that the model was broadly accurate in the long run when applied to large groups of people.

One economist who challenged the assumption of perfect rationality was the American Nobel Prize-winning economist Herbert Simon* who wrote several texts in the 1940s and 1950s suggesting that psychological factors constrained humans' ability to act in a fully rational way. Yet, in Thaler's words, "[Simon] had little impact on economics. And the reason is ... he didn't have systematic bias."[4] This is to say that Simon did not demonstrate that people would consistently act against the predictions of rational choice theory. Camerer and Loewenstein support Thaler's contention, saying that Simon's work "attracted attention, but did not alter the fundamental direction of economics."[5]

Academic Influences

Thaler's insight was that "there could be predictable bias."[6] By this he meant that sometimes people could consistently behave in a way that seemed "irrational" by the standards of rational choice theory.

He developed this idea from studying the work of Daniel Kahneman and Amos Tversky in the 1970s. During that decade, Kahneman and Tversky produced a series of seminal papers on human decision-making. Although Tversky died in 1996, Kahneman won the Nobel Prize in Economics in 2002 for "having integrated insights from psychological research into economic science, especially concerning human judgment and decision-making under uncertainty."[7] One of their influential articles was "Judgment under Uncertainty: Heuristics and Biases," published in the journal *Science** in 1974. It argued that people often used mental shortcuts—called "heuristics"*—to make judgments: for example, the "availability heuristic"* whereby people often rely on examples that immediately spring to mind when making a judgment. A person using this heuristic might overestimate the risk of dying from a heart attack because they can readily recall a friend with heart problems, even if the statistical probability is objectively low.

Another influential paper by Kahneman and Tversky was "Prospect Theory,"* published in the economics journal *Econometrica** in 1979. Its insight was that people treated money differently depending on whether it was a gain or a loss. Consider a coin toss— if heads, you win $20; if tails, you lose $20. Kahneman and Tversky found that most people would not take this bet. The participants in their experiments liked winning money, but strongly disliked losing it, a principle known as "loss aversion."*This contradicted the predictions of neoclassical assumptions, which assumed that people would treat gains and losses in the same way. The availability heuristic and loss aversion, and many other heuristics and biases, showed that people could systematically behave "irrationally."

In the 1980s, Thaler began collecting other examples of behavioral biases in a column called "Anomalies"* in the respected *Journal of Economic Perspectives*.*8 This column gave Thaler a small but influential platform to publicize the new field of behavioral economics to a mainstream economics audience. In Daniel Kahneman's view, "[Anomalies] got behavioral economics started as a field ... it became respectable."9

---

1. Colin Camerer and George Loewenstein, "Behavioral Economics: Past, Present, Future," in *Advances in Behavioral Economics*, ed. Colin Camerer et al. (Princeton, N. J.: Princeton University Press,

2003).

2. Richard H. Thaler and Cass R. Sunstein, *Nudge: Improving Decisions about Health, Wealth, and Happiness* (New York: Yale University Press, 2008), 6.

3. Gary Becker, "Irrational Behavior and Economic Theory," *Journal of Political Economy* 70, no. 1 (1962): 1–13.

4. Richard H. Thaler, "Do You Need a Nudge?" *Yale Insights*, November 4, 2009, accessed September 4, 2015, http://insights.som.yale.edu/insights/do-you-need-nudge.

5. Camerer and Loewenstein, "Behavioral Economics: Past, Present, Future," 5.

6. Thaler, "Do You Need a Nudge?"

7. "Sveriges Riksbank Prize in Economic Sciences in Memory of Alfred Nobel 2002," *Nobelprize. org*, accessed September 4, 2015, http://www.nobelprize.org/nobel_prizes/economic-sciences/laureates/2002/.

8. Richard H. Thaler's "Anomalies" columns are listed at http://faculty.chicagobooth.edu/Richard.Thaler/research/anomalies.html, accessed September 4, 2015.

9. Gregory Karp, "Profile: Richard H. Thaler, University of Chicago Booth School of Business Professor," *Chicago Tribune*, April 30, 2012, accessed September 4, 2015, http://articles.chicagotribune.com/2012–04–30/business/ct-biz–0430–executive-profile-thaler–20120430_1_economics-daniel-kahneman-cost-fallacy.

THE PROBLEM

KEY POINTS

- *Nudge* was motivated by a belief that rational choice theory,* with its assumptions that economic decisions are made rationally, was inadequate for understanding many human behaviors.
- Research in behavioral economics* suggested that people often made "irrational" errors in decision-making.
- Thaler and Sunstein synthesized hundreds of studies in *Nudge* to argue that the theories of behavioral economics could offer a more realistic understanding of human behavior.

Core Question

Richard H. Thaler and Cass R. Sunstein's *Nudge: Improving Decisions about Health, Wealth and Happiness* was motivated by the authors' belief that the models of neoclassical economics,* in which people made rational choices based on complete information, were inadequate for understanding many human behaviors. Instead they proposed that the theories of behavioral economics could provide a more realistic understanding of human decision-making.

Richard H. Thaler was trained in neoclassical economic thinking during his PhD in the 1970s. He regarded rational choice theory as a good model of how people should behave, but not an accurate description of how they often did behave in the real world. In his words, "if you want a single, unified theory of economic behavior we already have the best one available, the selfish, rational agent model ... the problem comes if, instead of trying to advise [people] how to make decisions, you are trying to predict what they will actually do."[1]

Thaler's skepticism is perhaps clarified by describing the full implications of perfect rationality. People do not make mistakes in a world of rational choice theory. They do not impulsively buy things they may later regret,[2] smoke when they want to quit,[3] fail to stick to diets,[4] choose a mortgage they cannot afford,[5] or open a business because of overconfidence.[6] They are immune to framing effects,[7] such as whether a hamburger is advertised as 90 percent fat or 10 percent fat-free. Social norms do not affect their judgment, like being told that 87 percent of people believe registering as an organ donor is the right thing to do.[8] Their minds are not susceptible to heuristics* and biases like loss aversion* (the tendency for people to more strongly prefer avoiding losses than receiving gains) or the availability heuristic* (a mental rule-of-thumb we use to evaluate how likely something is, based on how easily examples come to mind). Rational actors do not need help with their choices because they already make the best possible decision 100 percent of the time.

> "In many cases, people make pretty bad decisions—decisions they would not have made if they had paid full attention and possessed complete information, unlimited cognitive abilities, and complete self-control."
>
> —— Richard H. Thaler and Cass R. Sunstein, *Nudge: Improving Decisions about Health, Wealth, and Happiness*

The Participants

By the time Thaler and Sunstein were writing *Nudge* in the 2000s, behavioral economics had documented a large body of psychological evidence showing that people did in fact often behave "irrationally" by the standards of rational choice theory.

In the field of finance, Richard H. Thaler and the economist Werner De Bondt* found that psychological biases influenced the functioning of the stock market.[9] In 1997, the American economist David Laibson* introduced an influential model arguing that limits on self-control could make people less likely to save for retirement.[10] In 2001, the economists Brigitte Madrian* and Dennis Shea* demonstrated that changing default rules could affect major economic behaviors. They found that automatically enrolling a group of US employees into a certain pension plan, while allowing them the choice to opt out, dramatically increased the rate of participation in the program.[11] In 2008, the same year *Nudge* was published, the business professor John Beshears* and colleagues documented ways in which the market would not necessarily make people behave rationally, as assumed in neoclassical economics.[12]

The Contemporary Debate

In *Nudge,* Thaler and Sunstein synthesized the results of hundreds of scientific articles published over several decades. Throughout the book, they emphasize the long history and cross-disciplinary nature of behavioral economics by discussing the work of their many contemporaries and predecessors who contributed to the discipline's understanding of human behavior.

While the evidence of these psychological studies has now been accepted into mainstream economics, economists differ in their views about the implications of this evidence. One recent undergraduate economics textbook says that "research in behavioral economics suggests that the neoclassical rationality axiom does not stand up to tests of logic, experience, or the needs of society."[13] Another textbook has a more skeptical reaction, arguing that "markets tend to reward rational behavior, while punishing irrationality. Even if many participants do not behave rationally, those who do behave sensibly will have the biggest effect on prices and outcomes."[14] In other words, individual examples of irrationality may not add up to important effects in the overall population.

Lastly, the behavioral economists Colin Camerer* and George Loewenstein* offer a balanced perspective, saying that "at the core of behavioral economics is the conviction that increasing the realism of the psychological underpinnings of economic analysis will improve economics on its own terms—generating theoretical insights, making better predictions of field phenomena, and suggesting better policy. This conviction does not imply a wholesale rejection of the neoclassical approach."[15]

---

1. Richard H. Thaler, "When Will There Be a Single Unified 'Behavioral' Theory of Economic Activity?" in "What's the Question about Your Field That You Dread Being Asked?" *Edge*, March

28, 2013, accessed September 4, 2015, http://edge.org/conversation/whats-the-question-about-your-field-that-you-dread-being-asked#25056.

2. Richard H. Thaler and Cass R. Sunstein, *Nudge: Improving Decisions about Health, Wealth, and Happiness* (New York: Yale University Press, 2008), 51.

3. Thaler and Sunstein, *Nudge*, 44.

4. Thaler and Sunstein, *Nudge*, 7.

5. Thaler and Sunstein, *Nudge*, 134.

6. Thaler and Sunstein, *Nudge*, 32.

7. Thaler and Sunstein, *Nudge*, 36.

8. Thaler and Sunstein, *Nudge*, 182.

9. Werner De Bondt and Richard H. Thaler, "Does the Stock Market Overreact?" *Journal of Finance* 40, no. 3 (1985): 793–805.

10. David Laibson, "Golden Eggs and Hyperbolic Discounting," *Quarterly Journal of Economics* 112, no. 2 (1997): 443–78.

11. Brigitte Madrian and Dennis Shea, "The Power of Suggestion: Inertia in 401(k) Participation and Savings Behavior," *Quarterly Journal of Economics* 116, no. 4 (2001): 1149–87.

12. John Beshears et al., "How Are Preferences Revealed?" *Journal of Public Economics* 92 (2008): 1787–94.

13. Neva Goodwin et al., *Microeconomics in Context*, 3rd edn (Abingdon: Routledge, 2013), 155.

14. Hal Varian, *Intermediate Microeconomics,* 8th edn (New York: W. W. Norton & Company, 2009), 579.

15. Colin Camerer and George Loewenstein, "Behavioral Economics: Past, Present, Future," in *Advances in Behavioral Economics*, ed. Colin Camerer et al. (Princeton, NJ: Princeton University Press, 2003).

MODULE 4
THE AUTHORS' CONTRIBUTION

KEY POINTS

* Thaler and Sunstein's main argument in *Nudge* is that governments should help people to make better decisions without restricting their freedom of choice.

* Reconciling these contradictory goals was one of the main insights of *Nudge*.

* The author's philosophy of "libertarian paternalism"*—an idea founded on free choice (libertarianism*) and benevolent intervention (paternalism*)—built on work by themselves and their contemporaries in 2003.

Authors' Aims

Richard H. Thaler and Cass R. Sunstein use the opening chapters of *Nudge: Improving Decisions about Health, Wealth and Happiness* to establish that people's decision-making is often affected by psychological factors. They cite a large body of evidence showing that these factors can lead people to make poor decisions, supplementing this empirical evidence with anecdotes and personal observations about ways in which people think and behave irrationally.

After building their case, Thaler and Sunstein spell out its implications. They argue that governments should use the theories of behavioral economics* to help people make better decisions that would improve their lives. But they also stipulate that government intervention should not force people to make certain decisions, citing the words of the economist Milton Friedman* that people should be "free to choose."[1] They call this political philosophy "libertarian paternalism."

Nudge's concept of limited government intervention to improve individual decision-making was not entirely novel— a similar argument was made in a 2003 article by the behavioral economist Colin Camerer* and colleagues.[2] However, one great success of the book was its presentation of the idea of "soft paternalism" to a lay audience in accessible language, while supporting the concept's rationale with an overwhelming body of scientific evidence.

> "We argue for self-conscious efforts, by institutions in the private sector and also by government, to steer people's choices in directions that will improve their lives."
>
> —— Richard H. Thaler and Cass R. Sunstein, *Nudge: Improving Decisions about Health, Wealth, and Happiness*

Approach

Throughout *Nudge*, Thaler and Sunstein build their case for government intervention by citing the results of hundreds of scientific studies showing how psychological factors can negatively affect decision-making. Their combined expertise in behavioral economics and law made them well positioned to make this argument. Thaler was a founding figure in the field of behavioral economics and had systematically collected examples of deviations from rational behavior since the 1980s in his "Anomalies"* column in the *Journal of Economic Perspectives*.[3] Sunstein had written influential texts on how the principles of behavioral economics could apply to the law and explain people's interactions with the legal system. His expertise in governance and political philosophy helped provide *Nudge* with its coherent framework of government intervention.

Thaler and Sunstein first developed their ideas about government intervention in an article published in 2003 called "Libertarian Paternalism Is Not an Oxymoron."[4] This title highlighted an apparent contradiction. Libertarianism is a political philosophy that emphasizes individual liberty and is hostile to government oversight. To be paternalistic means to act on a person's behalf for what you deem to be their own good, like a parent who forbids their child from eating fast food. Thaler and Sunstein reconciled this contradiction through a subtle argument. They proposed that interventions to help people make better choices were permissible, provided they respected individual freedom of choice. They give the example of a firm that wishes to encourage its workers to save more.[5] Rather than asking them to enroll in a pension plan, the firm assumes that they will wish to participate. It automatically enrolls all employees unless they specifically choose to opt out. The general tendency of people to stick with a default increases the savings rate, while those who wish to opt out are free to do so.

Contribution in Context

Although Thaler and Sunstein did not modify their idea of libertarian paternalism when it was included in *Nudge* five years later, they did present it in a different context. In their book, Thaler and Sunstein are much more explicit in selling the idea of libertarian paternalism to American readers by framing it in the context of US politics. They say that their approach could "serve as a viable middle ground in our unnecessarily polarized society"[6] and act as a "real third way"*[7] that could appeal to both Democrats* and Republicans* (that is, to people at different points on the political spectrum).

Thaler and Sunstein were not the only behavioral economists to make this argument. In 2003, the same year they introduced libertarian paternalism, the behavioral economist Colin Camerer and colleagues published a paper that introduced "asymmetric paternalism."[8] The two philosophies are essentially identical, reflecting the fact that they come from a common school of thought. However, Camerer and colleagues were more direct in framing the potential political application of their philosophy, as indicated by the article's title "Regulation for Conservatives."* That title implicitly acknowledges that since political liberals tend to be more open to government interventions, arguments for "nudge"-like interventions may need to convince political conservatives in particular if they are to be broadly accepted.

---

1. Richard H. Thaler and Cass R. Sunstein, *Nudge: Improving Decisions about Health, Wealth, and Happiness* (New York: Yale University Press, 2008), 5.

2. Colin Camerer et al., "Regulation for Conservatives: Behavioral Economics and the Case for 'Asymmetric Paternalism,'" *University of Pennsylvania Law Review* 151, no. 3 (2003): 1211–54.
3. Richard H. Thaler's "Anomalies" columns are listed at http://faculty. chicagobooth.edu/Richard. Thaler/research/anomalies.html, accessed September 4, 2015.
4. Richard H. Thaler and Cass R. Sunstein, "Libertarian Paternalism Is Not an Oxymoron," *University of Chicago Law Review* 70, no. 4 (2003): 1159–1202.
5. Thaler and Sunstein, *Nudge*, 109.
6. Thaler and Sunstein, *Nudge*, 252.
7. Thaler and Sunstein, *Nudge*, 252.
8. Camerer et al., "Regulation for Conservatives."

SECTION 2
IDEAS

MAIN IDEAS

KEY POINTS

* There are two main themes in *Nudge*: how context can affect decision-making, and how governments can organize that context to help people make better choices without restricting freedom of choice.

* Thaler and Sunstein's main argument is that governments should "nudge"* people to make better decisions, as judged by the person themselves.

* The authors emphasize the applicability of their ideas to policy by providing specific examples of nudges in areas such as finance, health, and the environment.

Key Themes

Richard H. Thaler and Cass R. Sunstein's *Nudge: Improving Decisions about Health, Wealth and Happiness* is a book about human decision-making. In *Nudge*, Thaler and Sunstein examine two main themes on this topic:

* How context can affect decision-making
* How governments can organize that context to help people make better choices without restricting their freedom of choice.

Nudge's opening chapters describe the psychological factors that can sometimes affect decision-making; these include heuristics* (mental rules-of-thumb) and biases (tendencies toward certain interpretations of information), emotions and temptations, social pressures, and limits on cognitive ability (our ability to draw on our full intellectual capacity).

Thaler and Sunstein argue that as a result of these factors, the context in which people make choices often causes them to make poor decisions. Thaler and Sunstein's proposed solution is for governments to organize the choice environment, without banning any options, so that people are more likely to act in their own self-judged best interest. They call this approach "nudging."

> *"A nudge ... alters people's behavior in a predictable way without forbidding any options or significantly changing their economic incentives. To count as a mere nudge, the intervention must be easy and cheap to avoid ... Putting fruit at eye level counts as a nudge. Banning junk food does not."*
> —— Richard H. Thaler and Cass R. Sunstein, *Nudge: Improving Decisions about Health, Wealth, and Happiness*

Exploring the Ideas

The authors' main contention is that the context in which people make decisions can affect their choices. They give the example of an online government program that required senior citizens to choose one of 47 different prescription-drug plans.[1] This complexity made it very difficult to choose the optimal plan. Designing the environment to influence behavior is what Thaler and Sunstein call "choice architecture."*[2] They argue that governments should create better choice architecture to help people make good decisions in many areas of life. However, they also believe that governments should not coerce people by denying them freedom of choice.

Changing the choice architecture to encourage a certain behavior, without banning any options, is what Thaler and Sunstein call a "nudge." In their words, "a nudge ... alters people's behavior in a predictable way without forbidding any options or significantly changing their economic incentives."[3] Everyday examples of nudges include: a satellite navigation system that helps drivers to their destination, a sign encouraging people to take the stairs instead of the elevator, a statement using a social norm to encourage a certain behavior ("most people pay their tax on time"), and government nutritional guidelines. In the context of an online drug prescription website, one effective nudge automatically assigned people a plan based on their historical prescription usage, while allowing them the option to choose a different plan.[4]

Throughout *Nudge*, Thaler and Sunstein ground their arguments by providing anecdotal examples and empirical evidence from scientific studies. They also provide many specific, practical examples of how governments and firms can use nudging to improve people's decision-making.

One example is the US "Save More Tomorrow" program that,[5] motivated by theoretical research in behavioral economics,* suggests procrastination prevents people from arranging their retirement plans. This program asked a firm's employees to specify the percentage of their future wages they wanted to contribute to their retirement fund. As a result, when they received pay rises, their contribution automatically rose. This overcame the problem of inertia (inaction) because employees no longer needed to actively manage and update their pension arrangements whenever they received a raise.

Another example concerns organ donation. Although surveys indicate that many people support organ donation, few sign up as organ donors. Thaler and Sunstein argue that the bureaucratic steps necessary to register deter people from signing up. They propose that "mandated choice" could address this gap between people's intentions and their behaviors.[6] This could be implemented on occasions when people are already interacting with the government, such as during a driving-license application. At that point drivers would be required to check a box stating their organ-donation preferences.

A final example is energy efficiency. A key challenge in this area is that most consumers are not able to judge how energy-efficient things are. The authors highlight the usefulness of information-disclosure laws in this context, such as a law that requires car companies to post in large print the fuel economy of their vehicles.[7] This in turn nudges consumers to purchase more efficient vehicles, if they so desire.

Language and Expression

Nudge is an accessible work that simultaneously targets general readers, academics, and policy-makers. Thaler and Sunstein communicate their main ideas using simple and amusing anecdotal examples, and build support for their arguments by citing quantitative evidence from scientific studies. They conclude with specific suggestions of how nudging can apply to many different areas of policy-making in the United States.

The authors introduced three new concepts in *Nudge*: "nudging," "choice architecture," and "libertarian paternalism."* The first two refer to the way the decision environment can be organized to encourage certain behaviors. The last describes the philosophy behind nudging, reconciling the contradictory idea of government acting on a person's behalf while respecting their freedom of choice. All three terms have become well known in academic and policy circles, showing the extent of the book's influence.

---

1. Richard H. Thaler and Cass R. Sunstein, *Nudge: Improving Decisions about Health, Wealth, and Happiness* (New York: Yale University Press, 2008), 163.
2. Thaler and Sunstein, *Nudge*, 3.
3. Thaler and Sunstein, *Nudge*, 6.
4. Thaler and Sunstein, *Nudge*, 172.
5. Thaler and Sunstein, *Nudge*, 113.
6. Thaler and Sunstein, *Nudge*, 180.
7. Thaler and Sunstein, *Nudge*, 191.

MODULE 6
SECONDARY IDEAS

KEY POINTS

* There are two main secondary ideas in *Nudge*: that people use Automatic* (fast and instinctive) and Reflective (conscious and calculating) systems of thinking; and that people are already being constantly nudged* by the private sector.

* These ideas describe a mechanism for understanding how nudges work, and implicitly highlight a potential "dark side" of nudging.

* Thaler and Sunstein's argument that governments already nudge people through their existing choice architectures,* even if they do not intend to, may rebut a criticism the book later received.

Other Ideas

There are two main secondary ideas in Richard H. Thaler and Cass R. Sunstein's *Nudge: Improving Decisions about Health, Wealth and Happiness*:

* that people use Automatic and Reflective Systems of thinking

* that people experience nudges constantly in their day-to-day lives, whether the government intervenes or not.

The first idea is discussed early in *Nudge* as a way to frame the reader's understanding of how nudges work. Thaler and Sunstein discuss research from psychology and neuroscience that describes the functioning of the human brain. That approach conceives of two kinds of thinking: a fast and instinctive Automatic

System, and a slower, more rational Reflective System.[1] Many of the nudges Thaler and Sunstein cite throughout the book appear to work by targeting the Automatic System; in other words, by guiding people unconsciously rather than encouraging them to reflect more on their choices.

The second idea is that nudging is already pervasive in the real world in the form of advertising and sales techniques. Although Thaler and Sunstein only suggest nudges designed to improve human welfare, one subtext of the book is that it is easy to imagine "dark nudges" designed to encourage unhealthy habits or wasteful consumption.

> *"[Nudges] are the norm. We've been nudged forever. Eve and the serpent nudged Adam. Religions have been nudging us for thousands of years. Marketers nudge us. Ads are nudges. We can be nudged for good or for evil ... We don't claim to have invented nudges."*
>
> ——Richard H. Thaler, "Do You Need a Nudge?", *Yale Insights*

Exploring the Ideas

Thaler and Sunstein use the concepts "Econs* and Humans" in *Nudge* to contrast how neoclassical* and behavioral economics*— one representing the mainstream orthodox approach to Western economic policy, the other an integration of research in the field of psychology and economic theory—describe human behavior. "Econs" are the perfectly rational beings described in rational choice theory.* "Humans" are real people, who occasionally make irrational decisions. Early in *Nudge*, Thaler and Sunstein relate these concepts to an influential psychological theory that describes people as having two systems of thinking. These are called the "Automatic" and "Reflective" Systems.[2] Also known as System 1 and System 2, these are discussed in greater detail by the Israeli psychologist Daniel Kahneman* in his book *Thinking, Fast and Slow*.[3]

The Automatic System is fast and instinctive. It is driven by feelings, habits, and triggers in the environment, and requires little to no cognitive engagement. It is how "Humans" often think. Some examples of Automatic thinking are:

- Knowing the answer to 2 + 2 without thinking
- Immediately recognizing a person is angry by their tone of voice and body language
- Effortlessly understanding short sentences in your native language.

The Reflective System is deliberative and rational. It is driven by values, knowledge, and intentions, and requires cognitive engagement. It is how "Econs" always think. Some examples of Reflective thinking are:

- Calculating the answer to 391 × 624
- Deciding what to study at university
- Understanding sentences in a foreign language by listening to them slowly and carefully.

Nudges often change behavior by targeting the Automatic System. They therefore affect Humans (who use this system) but not Econs (who do not). Examples include changing a default rule to an option that most people will prefer, framing choices in ways that make them more appealing, and simplifying complex choices to make them more understandable. All these nudges reduce cognitive burden and, as Thaler and Sunstein put it, "make it easier for people to go their own way."[4]

Another secondary idea in *Nudge* is the pervasiveness of nudges in our daily lives. A subtext of this is that these "nudges" may not have one's best interests at heart. For example, one book review has called nudging "a marketer's dream."[5] Firms in sales and advertising have used some of the techniques described in *Nudge* for decades, in the form of product placements and celebrity endorsements. The American technology firm Apple's iBeacon product is an example of nudge techniques applied to modern advertising. The journalist Nina Zipkin describes how iBeacon can track the movements of customers in US stores via their smartphone, down to the location of the aisle they are standing in.[6] This information can be used to personalize a shopping experience by providing micro-level notifications about deals on products in the customer's eye-line.

Overlooked

One subtle argument Thaler and Sunstein make in *Nudge* is that governments are already nudging their citizens, even if they don't intend to. In their words, "choice architecture and its effects cannot be avoided."[7]

After the book's publication, this argument was overlooked

by critics who argued that *Nudge* was too paternalistic—that is, it proposed an excessive level of benevolent intervention in the life of the citizen. Sunstein's response was that "whenever a government has websites, communicates with its citizens, operates cafeterias, or maintains offices that people will visit, it nudges, whether or not it intends to."[8] His point was that existing choice architectures do not have a "neutral" default setting. One way or another, governments are already influencing their citizens' behavior through the structure of their existing institutions.

An implication of Sunstein's argument is that governments should therefore structure those institutions so that people are nudged toward better outcomes (as judged by themselves). Sunstein later expanded on this point in his book *Simpler*,[9] which discussed his three-year tenure as administrator of the Office of Information and Regulatory Affairs. In that book he emphasizes the importance of simplifying existing government forms and structures to improve their efficacy.

---

1. Richard H. Thaler and Cass R. Sunstein, *Nudge: Improving Decisions about Health, Wealth, and Happiness* (New York: Yale University Press, 2008), 19.

2. Thaler and Sunstein, *Nudge*, 19.

3. Daniel Kahneman, *Thinking, Fast and Slow* (New York: Farrar, Straus and Giroux, 2011).

4. Thaler and Sunstein, *Nudge*, 5.

5. Jeremy Waldron, "It's All for Your Own Good," *New York Review of Books*, October 9, 2014, accessed September 4, 2015, http://www.nybooks.com/articles/archives/2014/oct/09/cass-sunstein-its-all-your-own-good/.

6. Nina Zipkin, "Attention, Apple Shoppers: You're Being Followed," December 6, 2013, accessed

September 4, 2015, http://www.entrepreneur.com/article/230275.

7. Thaler and Sunstein, *Nudge*, 72.

8. Cass R. Sunstein, "There's a Backlash against Nudging—But It Was Never Meant to Solve Every Problem," *Guardian*, April 24, 2014, accessed September 4, 2015, http://www.theguardian.com/commentisfree/2014/apr/24/nudge-backlash-free-society-dignity-coercion.

9. Cass R. Sunstein, *Simpler: The Future of Government* (New York: Simon & Schuster, 2013).

MODULE 7
ACHIEVEMENT

KEY POINTS

* *Nudge* was well received by the public, academics, and policymakers.

* The book's success was helped by its impressive body of scientific evidence, its many practical examples of nudges,* and the timing of its publication.

* While nudges can improve decision-making, their main limitation is that they cannot address major societal challenges.

Assessing the Argument

In *Nudge: Improving Decisions about Health, Wealth, and Happiness*, Richard H. Thaler and Cass R. Sunstein make a convincing case that governments should "nudge" their citizens to make better decisions. The book's summary of decades of research from behavioral economics* and psychology, combined with its accessible writing style, helped make it a major success among the public, academics, and policy-makers.

The book's seemingly more realistic view of human decision-making contrasted with the more abstract, theoretical assumptions of neoclassical economics.* *Nudge*'s positive reception was likely encouraged by the fact that it was published in mid–2008, a time when many people regarded neoclassical economic thinking as discredited by its failure to predict that year's financial crisis, as noted in one book review.[1]

Within academia, the book's concepts of "choice architecture"* and "nudging" were quickly adopted by other disciplines interested in behavior change. For example, public-health researchers have examined whether nudging can improve the health of large populations by reducing smoking, obesity, and physical inactivity.[2] Marketers have applied the book's ideas to influencing consumer behavior,[3] and political scientists have examined whether nudging can encourage civic behavior, such as voting.[4]

> "Thaler and Sunstein have written an important book."
> —— Thomas C. Leonard, "Richard H. Thaler, Cass R. Sunstein, 'Nudge: Improving Decisions about Health, Wealth, and Happiness,'" *Constitutional Political Economy Book Review*

Achievement in Context

Nudge's ideas of light-touch government regulation and seemingly common-sense policy solutions appealed to many readers.[5] As well as being a popular best seller, Thaler and Sunstein's book affected real-world policy-making. Nudges were seen as particularly attractive policy options in the United Kingdom, partly because they were relatively cheap to implement at a time when the government was cutting spending in response to the 2008 financial crisis.*[6] The ideas contained in *Nudge* were quickly embraced by the right-wing Conservative party.* Three months after the book's publication, Conservative MP and future chancellor of the exchequer (financial minister) George Osborne* praised *Nudge* in the *Guardian* newspaper.[7] In 2010 the Conservative leader David Cameron,* by then prime minister, created the world's first Nudge

Unit* to help government officials implement the book's ideas. In the five years since its creation, the Nudge Unit has published several papers documenting its interventions in many different policy areas, including taxation, unemployment, and charitable giving, further emphasizing the book's impact.[8]

In the United States, the success of *Nudge* inspired the creation of the Social and Behavioral Sciences Team.* This group was formally created by an executive order of President Barack Obama* in September 2015 which stated that "research findings from fields such as behavioral economics and psychology about how people make decisions and act on them ... can be used to design government policies to better serve the American people."[9] That executive order was accompanied by a report describing the team's recent interventions. Some of their successful nudges include using personalized text messages to improve college enrollment rates among low-income students; simplifying governmental debt-collection letters to increase the number of people paying online; and improving the accuracy of self-reported sales figures by vendors selling goods to the government by requiring their signature at the top of an online form (thereby prompting more honest responses).[10]

Limitations

A key strength of *Nudge* is the universality of its concepts of "choice architecture" and "nudging." Because these relate to how people fundamentally make decisions, the book's ideas can easily apply to different countries and contexts.

Despite this strength, the concept of nudging is limited in one crucial way. Nudges must be "easy and cheap to avoid."[11] They do not allow more conventional policy tools like taxation and regulation. This limitation was highlighted in 2009 by the British politician Ed Miliband,* the future leader of the center-left Labour party,* who criticized the idea of nudge policies at a time when Britain was in recession. He argued that "*Nudge* was very fashionable ... for a few months before the financial crisis. *Nudge* was about not really needing the state to do big things ... People don't talk about *Nudge* much any more."[12]

While Miliband was arguably incorrect in his assessment that *Nudge* was just a passing fad, given the book's continued influence on policy-making in the UK and US in the years since he made his remarks, he was probably correct that nudges cannot match traditional policy tools for addressing major challenges like economic recessions. A useful contrast to the relatively incremental adjustments in policy suggested by *Nudge* is the $831 billion in economic stimulus the US government spent in response to the 2008 financial crisis. This intervention would have been forbidden under the principles of *Nudge*, as would other large-scale government responses to challenges like obesity and climate change.

---

1. Joel Anderson, "Review of *Nudge: Improving Decisions about Health, Wealth, and Happiness,*" *Economics and Philosophy* 26, no. 3 (2010): 369–76.

2. Theresa M. Marteau et al., "Judging Nudging: Can Nudging Improve Population Health?" *British Medical Journal* 342 (2011).

3. Daniel G. Goldstein et al., "Nudge Your Customers toward Better Choices," *Harvard Business Review*, December 2008, accessed September 4, 2015, https://hbr.org/2008/12/nudge-your-customers-toward-better-choices.

4. David W. Nickerson and Todd Rogers, "Do You Have a Voting Plan? Implementation Intentions, Voter Turnout, and Organic Plan Making," *Psychological Science* 21, no. 2 (2010): 194–9.

5. Benjamin M. Friedman, "Guiding Forces," *New York Times*, August 22, 2008, accessed September 5, 2015, http://www.nytimes.com/2008/08/24/books/review/Friedman-t.html?pagewanted=all&_r=0.

6. David Cameron, "The Next Age of Government," *TED*, February 2010, accessed September 4, 2015, http://www.ted.com/talks/david_ cameron?language=en.

7. George Osborne, "Nudge, Nudge, Win, Win," *Guardian*, July 14, 2008, accessed September 4, 2015, http://www.theguardian.com/commentisfree/2008/jul/14/conservatives.economy.

8. Behavioural Insights Team, "The Behavioural Insights Team Update report 2013–2015," accessed September 4, 2015, http://www. behaviouralinsights.co.uk/wp-content/uploads/2015/07/BIT_Update-Report-Final-2013–2015.pdf.

9. "Executive Order—Using Behavioral Science Insights to Better Serve the American People," The White House Office of the Press Secretary, September 15, 2015, accessed September 30, 2015, https://www.whitehouse.gov/the-press-office/2015/09/15/executive-order-using-behavioral-science-insights-better-serve-american.

10. Social and Behavioral Sciences Team, "Social and Behavioral Sciences Team Annual Report," Executive Office of the President National Science and Technology Council, September 2015, accessed September 30, 2015, https://www.whitehouse.gov/sites/default/files/microsites/ostp/sbst_2015_ annual_report_final_9_14_15.pdf.

11. Richard H. Thaler and Cass R. Sunstein, *Nudge: Improving Decisions about Health, Wealth, and Happiness* (New York: Yale University Press, 2008), 6.

12. Andrew Sparrow, "Fabian Conference—Live," *Guardian*, January 17, 2009, accessed September 4, 2015, http://www.theguardian.com/politics/blog/2009/jan/17/fabian-conference-blog.

PLACE IN THE AUTHORS' WORK

KEY POINTS

* Throughout their careers, Thaler and Sunstein have applied ideas from psychology and behavioral economics* to understanding human decision-making.

* Although Thaler and Sunstein were distinguished scholars before *Nudge*, the book hugely increased their profile and remains their biggest success.

* The book's accomplishment represented a culmination of Thaler's life's work by introducing the field of behavioral economics to a global audience.

Positioning

When *Nudge: Improving Decisions about Health, Wealth, and Happiness* was published in 2008, Richard H. Thaler and Cass R. Sunstein had each worked in academia for three decades. Both held professorships at the University of Chicago and had produced important and widely cited work, applying the principles of behavioral economics to finance and law. In spite of these achievements, *Nudge* was the biggest success of both authors' careers. It became an internationally acclaimed best seller, directly influenced government policy-making in some of the world's most advanced countries, and continues to be highly cited by many academic disciplines.

The ideas in *Nudge* reflected the authors' long-standing interest in applying theories from behavioral economics and psychology to improve human decision-making. In 1998, they collaborated with the American law professor Christine Jolls* to describe how behavioral economics could provide more realistic theories of law and government.[1] In 2003, they described how libertarian paternalism* could inform government policy-making in an article published in *The University of Chicago Law Review*.[2] That article, "Libertarian Paternalism Is Not an Oxymoron," concluded that their philosophy provided "a foundation for rethinking many areas of private and public law."[3]

Thaler and Sunstein later expanded their argument from that 44–page article into the 293 pages of *Nudge*. Their book-length treatment fleshed out their argument in several ways, giving a more complete description of the many psychological studies that informed their ideas about decision-making. They provided more examples of "nudges"* and described how the concept could be used in the context of American politics. The accessible language in the book also made it appealing to a non-academic audience.

> "Libertarian paternalism provides a basis for both understanding and rethinking a number of areas of contemporary law, including those aspects that deal with worker welfare, consumer protection, and the family."
>
> —— Richard H. Thaler and Cass R. Sunstein,
> "Libertarian Paternalism Is Not an Oxymoron,"
> *University of Chicago Law Review*

Integration

Thaler's overall body of work can be considered coherent. He has consistently written on behavioral economics throughout his career. Sunstein's writing is less unified because his academic interests are wide-ranging. He has published most frequently on law and governance but also on more esoteric topics such as animal rights, conspiracy theories, and political extremism. He is famously prolific—as of 2015 he is credited with almost 500 publications, including books, academic articles, and media pieces.

Bringing behavioral economics to global prominence, *Nudge* represents the culmination of Thaler's life's work. He is the author of many of the most important papers in the field and, in the 1980s and 1990s, introduced its ideas to a mainstream economics audience through his column "Anomalies"* in the *Journal of Economic Perspectives.** In consequence, the Nobel Prize-winning psychologist Daniel Kahneman* has called Thaler the "person who really created behavioral economics."[4] *Nudge's* best-selling, influential status confirmed the growth of behavioral economics from a discipline initially treated with contempt by many economists[5] to a respected field that offers important insights into human behavior.

Nudge is also an effective summary of Sunstein's body of work, examining how behavioral economics can inform theories of law and governance. The concept of nudging—which typically emphasizes incremental, case-specific modifications of existing policies—is consistent with Sunstein's writings on "judicial minimalism,"* a legal philosophy that favors case-by-case adjudication rather than major overhauls on matters of constitutional law.*

Significance

Many academics today consider Thaler a likely future winner of the Nobel Prize in Economics, based on work he had done before *Nudge* was published.[6] Sunstein is one of the most cited legal scholars in the world and was one of the highest officials of the Obama administration* during his three-year tenure as administrator of the Office of Information and Regulatory Affairs. Despite these existing accomplishments, the success of *Nudge* elevated both authors to a new global prominence.

Nudge's most dramatic real-world impact has been its effect on policy-making around the world. *Nudge*'s philosophy of light-touch regulation strongly appealed to the Conservative party* in the United Kingdom. In 2010, a mere two years after *Nudge* was published, David Cameron, prime minister of a Conservative-led administration, put the book's ideas into practice by creating the world's first governmental Nudge Unit.*The success of that group has since inspired the creation of the Social and Behavioral Sciences Team* in the United States and influenced policy-makers in Germany, the Netherlands, Finland, Singapore, and Australia.[7]

The ideas in *Nudge* also inspired the creation of the "world's first public policy behavioural insights conference" in 2014.[8] The success of the Behavioural Exchange conference, now an annual event, is a clear sign of the continuing interest in *Nudge* from academics, policymakers, and the media.

1. Christine Jolls et al., "A Behavioral Approach to Law and Economics," *Stanford Law Review* 50, no. 5 (1998): 1471–550.

2. Richard H. Thaler and Cass R. Sunstein, "Libertarian Paternalism Is Not an Oxymoron," *University of Chicago Law Review* 70, no. 4 (2003).

3. Sunstein and Thaler, "Libertarian Paternalism," 1202.

4. Morgan Housel, "Daniel Kahneman on Challenging Economic Assumptions," *Motley Fool*, June 29, 2013, accessed September 4, 2015, http://www.fool. com/investing/general/2013/06/29/challenging-assumptions-an-economist-considers-psy.aspx.

5. Housel, "Daniel Kahneman on Challenging Economic Assumptions."

6. Noah Smith, "Five Economists Who Deserve Nobels," *Bloomberg View*, December 9, 2014, accessed September 4, 2015, http://www.bloombergview.com/articles/2014–12–09/five-economists-who-deserve-nobels.

7. Behavioural Insights Team, "The Behavioural Insights Team Update Report 2013–2015," accessed September 4, 2015, http://www.behaviouralinsights.co.uk/wp-content/uploads/2015/07/BIT_Update-Report-Final–2013-2015.pdf.

8. Behavioural Insights Team, "Behavioural Exchange 2014," accessed September 30, 2015, http://www.behaviouralinsights.co.uk/bx2015/behavioural-exchange–2014/.

SECTION 3
IMPACT

MODULE 9
THE FIRST RESPONSES

KEY POINTS

* *Nudge* received two main criticisms: that nudges* were too paternalistic; that nudges could only change behavior in a superficial way.
* Thaler and Sunstein responded to their critics through interviews and articles.
* Thaler and Sunstein conceded that nudging alone could not fix major societal problems, but they did not change their essential positions.

Criticism

Richard H. Thaler and Cass R. Sunstein's *Nudge: Improving Decisions about Health, Wealth and Happiness* became an international best seller and was named one of the best books of 2008 by the British periodical the *Economist*[1] and by the *Financial Times*[2] newspaper. Despite its success, *Nudge* also received criticism from media figures and academics.

The first criticism was that nudging was too paternalistic, as exemplified in an argument between Thaler and the American economist Richard Posner* shortly after *Nudge* was published. The point of contention was the US Consumer Financial Protection Agency,* a body set up in response to the 2008 financial crisis.* Influenced by research in behavioral economics, one of its goals was to protect consumers from financial abuse by using "actual data about how people make financial decisions."[3] It required financial institutions to offer customers simple "vanilla" (that is, unchallenging and "everyday") mortgages whose conditions could be read in less than three minutes. Posner harshly criticized this proposal in the *Wall Street Journal*.[4] He argued that vanilla products would make sellers fearful of offering other types of mortgages. This would reduce competition in the market and make customers worse off.

The second critique was that nudges were too superficial to address major societal challenges. This criticism was detailed in a report on behavior change by the House of Lords (the higher of the British Parliament's two governmental law-making bodies). Baroness Julia Neuberger,* heading that report, argued that serious behavior change required "more than just nudge ... behavioural change interventions appear to work best when they're part of a package of regulation and fiscal measures."[5] The report cited obesity as a societal challenge influenced by complex social and environmental factors that should therefore be addressed by a combination of policy measures rather than just individual-level nudges.[6]

> "Our central finding is that non-regulatory measures used in isolation, including 'nudges,' are less likely to be effective. Effective policies often use a range of interventions."
>
> —— House of Lords Science and Technology Select Committee, "Behaviour Change Report"

Responses

Since *Nudge*'s publication, Thaler and Sunstein have responded to their critics through a large number of interviews and articles.

Thaler rejected Posner's argument over mortgages as misleading, in an article published in *PBS Newshour*.[7] He argued that vanilla financial products would not restrict consumer choice but would provide a baseline against which customers could judge other products. Firms would be free to offer more complicated products for people who wanted them. Thaler compared the idea of a vanilla mortgage to the standard lease used in rental agreements that provides a framework for consumers to identify whether a landlord is offering them unusual terms. This frame of reference helps them to judge whether the nonstandard terms are in their best interest.

In a *Guardian* article, Sunstein acknowledged that nudging alone could not fix society's biggest challenges, saying, "nudges are not a sufficient approach to some of our most serious problems, such as violent crime, poverty, and climate change ... No one denies that requirements and bans have their place."[8] Thaler and Sunstein have never themselves claimed nudging could solve these kinds of problems. This criticism may be more fairly directed at policy-makers who neglect conventional policy tools, like taxation and regulation, in favor of nudging because the former are more difficult to implement.

Conflict and Consensus

Thaler and Sunstein countered many initial criticisms of *Nudge* by carefully reiterating the book's core arguments. They repeated that true nudges did not restrict freedom of choice and that policymakers who did so were not adhering to libertarian paternalism. They admitted that nudges alone could not solve all of society's problems—but they themselves had never made this claim.

Subsequent debates advanced subtler arguments that were not as easily refuted. One criticism was that nudges often exploit the same flaws in decision-making that they were designed to ameliorate. In other words, nudges often work by targeting the fast and instinctive Automatic System* instead of the slow and deliberative Reflective System. This point was raised in a review of *Nudge* in the *New York Review of Books*.[9] The reviewer concluded that he would prefer nudges that made him a consciously better chooser rather than an unconsciously guided one. Although Sunstein responded to the author's other criticisms, he did not address this point.[10]

1. "Pick of the Pile," *Economist*, December 4, 2008, accessed September 4, 2015, http://www.economist.com/node/12719711.

2. "Best Business Books," *Financial Times*, 2008, accessed September 4, 2015, http://ig.ft.com/sites/business-book-award/books/2008/longlist/nudge-by-richard-thaler-and-cass-sunstein.

3. "Executive Summary of Financial Regulatory Reform: A New Foundation," US Treasury Department, June 17, 2009, accessed September 4, 2015, http://www.treasury.gov/initiatives/wsr/Documents/executive_summary.pdf.

4. Richard Posner, "Treating Financial Consumers as Consenting Adults," *Wall Street Journal*, July 22, 2009, accessed September 4, 2015, http://www.wsj.com/articles/SB10001424052970203946904574302213213148166.

5. Elizabeth Day, "Julia Neuberger: 'A Nudge in the Right Direction Won't Run the Big Society,'" *Observer*, July 17, 2011, accessed September 4, 2015, http://www.theguardian.com/society/2011/

jul/17/julia-neuberger-nudge-big-society.

6. House of Lords Science and Technology Select Committee, "Behaviour Change Report," *HL Paper* 179, (2011): 52–7, accessed September 4, 2015, http://www.publications.parliament.uk/pa/ld201012/ldselect/ldsctech/179/179.pdf.

7. Richard H. Thaler, "Thaler Responds to Posner on Consumer Protection," *PBS Newshour*, July 28, 2009, accessed September 4, 2015, http://www.pbs.org/newshour/making-sense/thaler-responds-to-posner-on-c/.

8. Cass R. Sunstein, "There's a Backlash against Nudging—But It Was Never Meant to Solve Every Problem," *Guardian*, April 24, 2014, accessed September 4, 2015, http://www.theguardian.com/commentisfree/2014/apr/24/nudge-backlash-free-society-dignity-coercion.

9. Jeremy Waldron, "It's All for Your Own Good," New York Review of Books, October 9, 2014, accessed September 4, 2015, http://www.nybooks.com/articles/archives/2014/oct/09/cass-sunstein-its-all-your-own-good/.

10. Cass R. Sunstein, "Nudges: Good and Bad," New York Review of Books, October 23, 2014, accessed September 4, 2015, http://www.nybooks.com/articles/archives/2014/oct/23/nudges-good-and-bad/.

MODULE 10
THE EVOLVING DEBATE

KEY POINTS

* The term "nudging"* is now commonly used by academics and global policymakers.

* Sunstein's book *Why Nudge?* summarizes the authors' responses to the criticisms the book has accumulated.

* The success of *Nudge* has led to many interventions being incorrectly described as "behavioral economics."* There is now a move toward broader terms such as "behavioral science"* and "behavioral insights."

Uses and Problems

Richard H. Thaler and Cass R. Sunstein's argument in *Nudge: Improving Decisions about Health, Wealth, and Happiness* that governments should nudge their citizens has been broadly accepted by many policymakers and academics. There are two noticeable trends in the current debate.

The first is the continued critiques of the book's ideas. One criticism by the Belgian philosopher Luc Bovens* is that nudges are dangerous because they are subtle.[1] People do not notice them in the way they notice bans or regulation, so bad nudges might not trigger the same political response as bad regulations. Another criticism is that *Nudge* identifies consistent flaws in human decision-making—but policymakers are, of course, subject to the same flaws. How, then, can the public trust them to make sensible interventions?[2] A further criticism is that because nudges are designed to discourage people from making bad choices, they make it less likely that people will learn from their mistakes.

Sunstein's book *Why Nudge?*[3] contains his responses to the long list of criticisms *Nudge* has received. The American psychologist Barry Schwartz* concluded in his review of *Why Nudge?* that it was "nuanced and sophisticated in its arguments."[4]

The second trend is an unexpected consequence of *Nudge*'s enormous success—behavior change has become too closely identified with behavioral economics in the popular media. Daniel Kahneman* discusses this in *The Behavioral Foundations of Public Policy*.[5] For him, many applications of cognitive and social psychology to policy have been incorrectly called "behavioral economics." Thaler himself, he adds, "has always insisted on a narrow definition of behavioral economics and ... would prefer to see 'nudges' described as applications of behavioral science."[6]

This may seem just a superficial debate about labeling. Its broader implication is that the success of *Nudge* has legitimized the ability of psychology, and other disciplines in the social sciences, to contribute to policy-making. However, this represents a major shift, given that economics has traditionally been the only academic field that seriously affects policy-making. There are now conscious

> "The whole point of a nudge, and of creating the Behavioural Insights Teams in the UK and now others around the world, was to give non-economists a voice in designing policy."
> —— Richard H. Thaler quoted in Peter Ubel, "Q & A with Richard H. Thaler on What It Really Means to Be a 'Nudge,'" *Forbes*

efforts to use broader terms such as "behavioral science" to describe behavioral change interventions.

Schools of Thought

Nudge has achieved the status of a distinct school of thought. The term "nudging" has entered the language of academics and policymakers, and some of the most influential organizations in the world now apply the book's ideas. For example, the report *Mind, Society and Behavior* from the Washington-based global financial institution the World Bank* discusses how nudging can be used in the developing world in areas like microfinance (a type of financial service targeted at individuals and small groups who lack access to traditional banking services) and testing for HIV (the virus that causes the immune system disease AIDS).[7] In 2013 the Financial Conduct Authority,* the UK's financial regulator, published a report describing how behavioral economics and nudging inform its work.[8] The behavioral economist Pete Lunn* has written for the Organization for Economic Co-operation and Development (OECD*)—a group of countries that promote democracy and economic growth by means of the market economy system—on the topic of behavioral economics and regulatory policy (policy formulated for purposes such as responding to financial crises or planning public investment).[9]

The 5,000 citations *Nudge* has received is a clear sign of its influence in the academic world.[10] Even more impressively, these citations have come from a diverse set of disciplines, including economics, psychology, public health, marketing, sociology, medicine, political science, criminology, and philosophy.

In Current Scholarship

The most influential group disseminating the ideas of *Nudge* today
is arguably the Behavioural Insights Team* in the United Kingdom.
This group—also called the Nudge Unit—was set up by Prime
Minister David Cameron* in 2010 to implement the book's ideas
in the new Conservative-led government. Richard H. Thaler is an
external advisor to the team, demonstrating his continued influence.

The group's stated objectives are clearly inspired by
Nudge. These are to "[enable] people to make 'better choices for
themselves'," to "make public services more cost-effective and
easier for citizens to use," and to "[introduce] a more realistic
model of human behaviour to policy."[11] However, there are also
signs that while the group has adopted the ideas of *Nudge*, it is not
defined by them. On their website, the team do not use the word
"nudge" to describe their approach, and their formal name uses the
more general term "behavioural insights" instead of "behavioral
economics." This mirrors the trend discussed by Kahneman of
moving toward a broader approach to behavioral interventions that
is not tied to the ideas of behavioral economics.

---

1. Luc Bovens, "The Ethics of Nudge," in *Preference Change: Approaches from Philosophy, Economics
and Psychology*, ed. Till Grüne-Yanoff and Sven Ove Hansson (New York: Springer, 2009), 207–19.
2. Jan Schnellenbach and Christian Schubert, "Behavioral Political Economy: A Survey," *European
Journal of Political Economy* (2015).

3. Cass R. Sunstein, *Why Nudge?* (New York: Yale University Press, 2014).

4. Barry Schwartz, "Why Not Nudge? A Review of Cass R. Sunstein's *Why Nudge?*" *thepsychreport,* April 17, 2014, accessed September 4, 2015, http://thepsychreport.com/essays-discussion/nudge-review-cass-sunsteins-why-nudge/.

5. Eldar Shafir, ed., *The Behavioral Foundations of Public Policy* (Princeton, N. J.: Princeton University Press, 2012), 7.

6. Shafir, *Behavioural Foundations*, 7.

7. World Bank, "Mind, Society, and Behavior," *World Bank Group Flagship Report*, 2015, accessed September 26, 2015, http://www.worldbank.org/content/dam/Worldbank/Publications/WDR/WDR%202015/WDR-2015-Full-Report.pdf.

8. Kristine Erta et al., "Applying Behavioural Economics at the Financial Conduct Authority," *FCA Occasional Paper* no. 1 (2013), accessed September 4, 2015, https://www.fca.org.uk/static/documents/occasional-papers/occasional-paper-1.pdf.

9. Pete Lunn, *Regulatory Policy and Behavioural Economics* (Paris: OECD Publishing, 2014).

10. Google Scholar records 5,495 texts which have cited *Nudge* as of September 26, 2015: https://scholar.google.com/scholar?cites= 16854468477297806637&as_sdt=2005&sciodt=0,5&hl=en.

11. Behavioural Insights Team, "Who We Are," accessed September 4, 2015, http://www.behaviouralinsights.co.uk/about-us/.

IMPACT AND INFLUENCE TODAY

KEY POINTS

* *Nudge* has become a key reference for anyone interested in decision-making and public policy.
* By highlighting the contributions of behavioral economics* and psychology to understanding human behavior, the book challenges the dominance of neoclassical economics* as the only discipline capable of influencing policy.
* While *Nudge* has received criticism, its ideas have mostly been accepted by policymakers, business people, and academics.

Position

Less than 10 years after the publication of Richard H. Thaler and Cass R. Sunstein's *Nudge: Improving Decisions about Health, Wealth, and Happiness*, the book has become a key reference text for people in policy, academia, and business who are interested in decision-making and behavior change. Although *Nudge* has received considerable criticism, this is partly because the book's success and global influence have made it a very visible target. Sunstein's comprehensive response to these criticisms in *Why Nudge?* suggests that the ideas of choice architecture* and nudging* will continue to be influential for years to come.

Nudge has challenged the traditional dominance of neoclassical economics in policy-making. Despite their prominence in the field of behavioral economics, both Thaler and Sunstein have argued that psychological research in general should play a greater role in policy debates. Sunstein makes this point by highlighting that the US president has a Council of Economic Advisers, but not a Council of Psychological Advisers.[1] To this end both have argued for the use of the broader term "behavioral science."*

> "Politicians will only succeed if they ... treat people as they are, rather than as they would like them to be. If you combine this very simple, very conservative thought—go with the grain of human nature—with all the advances in behavioral economics ... I think we can achieve a real increase in well-being, in happiness, in a stronger society."
>
> ——David Cameron, "Next Age of Government," TED

Interaction

The success of *Nudge* and its promotion of behavioral science has dramatically affected policy-making in the United Kingdom. Between 2010 and 2015 the Behavioural Insights Team* (the Nudge Unit) published over a dozen papers documenting its *Nudge*-inspired interventions in policy areas such as the labor market, energy use, fraud, taxation, organ donation, and charitable giving. Some of its successes include:

- Generating millions of pounds in additional tax revenue by rewriting tax letters to include phrases like "Nine out of ten people in your town pay their taxes on time."[2] This intervention drew on research from psychology about how social norms affect behavior.
- Designing a successful program to help unemployed

individuals return to employment. This program asked job-seekers to specify how they would search for a job instead of reporting on what activities they had undertaken. It also included an expressive writing component that asked individuals to identify their personal strengths.[3]

- Increasing the number of organ donors in the UK by nudging people to sign up after they renewed their driving licenses online.[4]

The success of the Behavioral Insights Team has provided a major publicity boost to the concept of policy-making that is informed by behavioral science and scientific methodology. The group's director, David Halpern,* has indicated that he sees their approach as the way of the future, saying, "I think we'll look back on this in a decade or two and say,'You mean we didn't use to do this?'"[5]

The Continuing Debate

Nudge has produced diverse responses in the academic world. The British health psychologist Susan Michie* has been a noted critic of the limitations of nudging for changing health behaviors. She highlights that behaviors such as smoking and obesity are usually influenced by community- and population-level factors, rather than just the individual factors that nudging typically targets. For example, nudging an obese person to drink less soda may be ineffective for weight loss if the person lives in an environment that encourages unhealthy eating. Michie has introduced the Behaviour Change Wheel that provides a more detailed framework for designing interventions by taking into account these multi-level factors.[6]

How has mainstream economics reacted to *Nudge*? The book is rooted in the field of behavioral economics, which evolved as a response to the unrealistic assumptions about human behavior made in neoclassical economics. Kahneman* has said "the assumptions have been challenged, but economics is still pretty much the same discipline it was."[7] This may be too pessimistic. The behavioral economists Colin Camerer* and George Loewenstein* argue that behavioral economics is not a revolution that will replace neoclassical economics; instead, its ideas will be absorbed into neoclassical economic thinking.[8] Perhaps the most valuable change it has made is to suggest that the "one size fits all" rational actor* model, according to which we make economic decisions rationally in the light of the information we possess, is not always an appropriate tool for understanding human behavior. In Thaler's view, "just as psychology has no unified theory ... so behavioral economics will have a multitude of theories."[9] Ultimately, given that *Nudge* was published less than a decade ago, its long-term influence on mainstream economics remains to be seen.

1. Cass R. Sunstein, "The Council of Psychological Advisers," *Annual Review of Psychology*, accessed September 4, 2015, http://dash.harvard.edu/bitstream/handle/1/13031653/annualreview9_15.pdf?sequence=1.
2. Behavioural Insights Team, "Applying Behavioural Insights to Reduce Fraud, Error and Debt," February 2012, accessed September 4, 2015, https://www.gov.uk/government/uploads/system/

uploads/attachment_data/file/60539/BIT_FraudErrorDebt_accessible.pdf.

3. Katrin Bennhold, "Britain's Ministry of Nudges," *New York Times*, December 7, 2013, accessed September 4, 2015, http://www.nytimes.com/2013/12/08/business/international/britains-ministry-of-nudges.html?_r=0.

4. Behavioural Insights Team, "Applying Behavioural Insights to Charitable Giving," accessed September 4, 2015, https://www.gov.uk/government/uploads/system/uploads/attachment_data/file/203286/BIT_Charitable_ Giving_Paper.pdf.

5. Bennhold, "Britain's Ministry of Nudges."

6. Susan Michie et al., "The Behaviour Change Wheel: A New Method for Characterising and Designing Behaviour Change Interventions," *Implementation Science* 6, no. 42 (2011).

7. Morgan Housel, "Daniel Kahneman on Challenging Economic Assumptions," *Motley Fool*, June 29, 2013, accessed September 4, 2015, http://www.fool.com/investing/general/2013/06/29/challenging-assumptions-an-economist-considers-psy.aspx.

8. Colin Camerer and George Loewenstein, "Behavioral Economics: Past, Present, Future," in *Advances in Behavioral Economics*, ed. Colin Camerer et al. (Princeton, NJ: Princeton University Press, 2003).

9. Richard H. Thaler, "When Will There Be a Single Unified 'Behavioral' Theory of Economic Activity?" in "What's the Question about Your Field That You Dread Being Asked?" *Edge*, March 28, 2013, accessed September 4, 2015, http://edge.org/conversation/whats-the-question-about-your-field-that-you-dread-being-asked#25056.

MODULE 12
WHERE NEXT?

KEY POINTS

* *Nudge* will likely continue to stimulate interest from academics and policymakers all over the world.

* The most significant long-term impact of *Nudge* may be to promote a norm of governance based on science.

* Bringing behavioral economics* to global prominence and promoting evidence-based policy-making has been the seminal contribution of *Nudge*.

Potential

Richard H. Thaler and Cass R. Sunstein's *Nudge: Improving Decisions about Health, Wealth, and Happiness* will likely continue to stimulate academic research in a diverse set of disciplines. It is a standard reference text on university courses in behavioral economics and has been cited by thousands of papers and reports. In the world of policy, the book's ideas have attracted interest from organizations as diverse as the World Bank,[*1] the OECD,[*2] the House of Lords (the upper chamber of the British Parliament),[3] and the governments of the United States, the United Kingdom, Germany, the Netherlands, Finland, Singapore, and Australia.[4] The list of policy areas *Nudge* has influenced is equally comprehensive, including tax collection, finance, immigration, charitable giving, energy efficiency and sustainability, criminality and fraud, unemployment, education, cybersecurity, and international development.[5]

"One of our main hopes is that an understanding of choice architecture, and the power of nudges, will lead others to think of creative ways to improve human lives in other domains."

— Richard H. Thaler and Cass R. Sunstein, *Nudge: Improving Decisions about Health, Wealth, and Happiness*

Future Directions

In the long term, the most significant contributions of *Nudge* may be its promotion of two norms of science-based policy-making.

The first is that policy-makers should use the best available science to design their interventions. This may mean using more than just the ideas in *Nudge*, which only suggests a relatively narrow spectrum of intervention types constrained by the principles of behavioral economics and libertarian paternalism.* This trend has already begun. The formal names of the UK and US Nudge Units do not use the words "nudge"* or "behavioral economics." They are called the Behavioural Insights Team* and the Social and Behavioral Sciences Team.* "Behavioral insights" and "social and behavioral sciences" are broad terms. These names allow these groups the freedom to use diverse sources of scientific evidence and different tools of intervention rather than just those discussed in *Nudge*.

The second norm is that policymakers should consistently test the effectiveness of their interventions using gold-standard scientific methods like randomized controlled trials,* or RCTs (a method used in the social sciences to determine the effectiveness of an intervention). This trend has already begun. In 2012 the UK Nudge Unit and a group of academics published "Test, Learn, Adapt," a report that argued UK policymakers should use RCTs to test the effectiveness of their interventions.[6] The Obama administration* in the US has also embraced RCTs, saying that government must use "rigorous evidence and evaluation to ensure that [it] makes smart investments with taxpayer funds."[7] Thaler, too, has spoken of the need to use RCTs in policy-making, saying that "you can't make evidence-based policy decisions without evidence."[8]

This norm is directly promoted by the Behavioural Insights Team in the UK and the Social and Behavioral Sciences Team in the US, whose annual reports meticulously document how their interventions are conducted and evaluated. The economist Justin Wolfers noted his approval of this trend in a *NewYorkTimes* commentary, saying that "the big idea is ... not about knowing how to do better, it's about testing what works. Experiment relentlessly, keep what works, and discard what doesn't. Following this recipe may yield a government that's ... clear, user-friendly and unflinchingly effective."[9]

While *Nudge* did not create either of these norms, its global success and emphasis on evidence-based policy has shone a spotlight on their importance.

Summary

Nudge made a convincing argument that governments could improve their citizens' lives without restricting their freedom of choice. It used evidence from behavioral economics and psychology to support this argument and gave specific, sensible suggestions on how policymakers could apply its ideas. Its global influence represents a major success for the field of behavioral economics and its theories of human decision-making.

The rise of behavioral economics mirrors the changing reputation of *Nudge* co-author Richard H. Thaler among mainstream economists. To quote the Harvard economist David Laibson,* "during most of the 1980s [Thaler] was dismissed as a crank ... It takes a lot of courage to get a decade of rejection and to stick to your guns. [Thaler] kept fighting, and eventually almost everyone came around to his view."[10] In 2015, Thaler became president of the American Economic Association, a sign of how his once-radical views have been accepted into mainstream economics.

---

1. World Bank, "Mind, Society, and Behavior," *World Bank Group Flagship Report*, 2015, accessed September 26, 2015, http://www.worldbank.org/content/dam/Worldbank/Publications/WDR/WDR%202015/WDR–2015-Full-Report.pdf.

2. Pete Lunn, *Regulatory Policy and Behavioural Economics* (Paris: OECD Publishing, 2014).

3. House of Lords Science and Technology Select Committee, "Behaviour Change," *HL Paper* 179 (2011), accessed September 4, 2015, http://www. publications.parliament.uk/pa/ld201012/ldselect/ldsctech/179/179.pdf.

4. Behavioural Insights Team, "The Behavioural Insights Team Update Report 2013–2015," accessed September 4, 2015, http://www.behaviouralinsights.co.uk/wp-content/uploads/2015/07/BIT_Update-Report-Final–2013–2015.pdf.

5. Behavioural Insights Team, "Update Report 2013–2015."

6. Laura Haynes et al. "Test, Learn, Adapt: Developing Public Policy with Randomised Controlled Trials," *Cabinet Office*, June 2012, accessed September 4, 2015, https://www.gov.uk/government/

uploads/system/uploads/attachment_data/file/62529/TLA-1906126.pdf.

7. Tom Kalil, "Funding What Works: The Importance of Low-Cost Randomized Controlled Trials," *White House Blog*, July 9, 2014, accessed September 4, 2015, https://www.whitehouse.gov/ blog/2014/07/09/funding-what-works-importance-low-cost-randomized-controlled-trials.

8. Richard H. Thaler, "Watching Behavior before Writing the Rules," *New York Times*, July 7, 2012, accessed September 4, 2015, http://www.nytimes. com/2012/07/08/business/behavioral-science-can-help-guide-policy-economic-view.html.

9. Justin Wolfers, "A Better Government, One Tweak at a Time," *New York Times*, September 25, 2015, accessed September 30, 2015, http://www. nytimes.com/2015/09/27/upshot/a-better-government-one-tweak-at-a-time. html?rref=upshot&_r=0.

10. Gregory Karp, "Profile: Richard H. Thaler, University of Chicago Booth School of Business Professor," *Chicago Tribune*, April 30, 2012, accessed September 4, 2015, http://articles. chicagotribune.com/2012–04–30/business/ct-biz-0430-executive-profile-thaler–20120430_1_ economics-daniel-kahneman-cost-fallacy.

GLOSSARY OF TERMS

1. **"Anomalies":** the title of Richard H. Thaler's influential column in the *Journal of Economic Perspectives* during the 1980s and 1990s. He used this column as a platform to introduce the ideas of behavioral economics to a mainstream economic audience.

2. **Automatic and Reflective systems:** a theory based on research in psychology and neuroscience that conceives of two distinct types of human thinking: the fast and instinctive Automatic System, and the more ponderous and calculating Reflective System.

3. **Availability heuristic:** a mental rule-of-thumb according to which people use examples that come readily to mind when making a judgment.

4. **Behavioral economics:** a subdiscipline of economics that integrates findings from psychology into models of economic decision-making.

5. **Behavioral science:** a broad term that includes the ideas of behavioral economics, psychology, and other academic disciplines that contribute to an understanding of human behavior.

6. **Behavioural Insights Team:** an influential group established in the United Kingdom by Prime Minister David Cameron in 2010 to implement the ideas of *Nudge* within government.

7. **Chicago school:** a neoclassical economic school of thought that is associated with the University of Chicago economics department.

8. **Choice architecture:** the context in which people make decisions.

9. **Cognitive bias:** a way of interpreting the world that can cause systematic deviations from rational judgments and behavior.

10. **Conservative party:** a right-wing political party in the United Kingdom, founded in 1834.

11. **Constitutional law:** a body of law derived from a country's written constitution.

12. **Consumer Financial Protection Agency:** a US government agency established in 2011, responsible for consumer protection in the finance sector.

13. **Democratic party:** one of the two main political parties in the United States.

Founded in 1828, it is associated with center-left politics.

14. *Econometrica*: one of the most prestigious journals in the field of economics, in publication since 1933.

15. **Econs and Humans:** the terms Thaler and Sunstein used to distinguish between ideal decision-makers in economic models (Econs) and people who make decisions in the real world (Humans).

16. **Financial Conduct Authority:** a regulatory body in the United Kingdom that monitors the financial services industry.

17. **Heuristic:** a mental rule-of-thumb used in decision-making.

18. *Journal of Economic Perspectives*: an economic journal covering a broad range of topics, in publication since 1987.

19. **Judicial minimalism:** a philosophy that advocates incremental interpretations of American constitutional law.

20. **Labour party:** a center-left political party in the United Kingdom.

21. **Libertarianism:** a political philosophy that emphasizes individual liberty and freedom of choice.

22. **Libertarian paternalism:** the philosophy discussed in *Nudge*. Thaler and Sunstein describe it as a "soft" paternalism that encourages people to act in their own best interest without restricting their freedom of choice.

23. **Loss aversion:** the tendency for people to favor avoiding loss over receiving gain.

24. **Neoclassical economics:** the mainstream synthesis of economic thought developed after World War II. It assumes a model of human behavior in which people have rational preferences and act on the basis of complete information.

25. **Nudge:** any aspect of choice architecture that changes people's behavior in a predictable way, and is cheap and easy to avoid.

26. **Nudge Unit:** the informal name of the Behavioural Insights Team.

27. **Obama administration:** the government of US President Barack Obama, in office since January 2009 and scheduled to remain in power until January 2017.

28. **OECD:** the Organization for Economic Co-operation and Development, a group of countries that promote democracy and economic growth via the market economy system.

29. **Paternalism:** a type of behavior by an individual or group that restricts a person's freedom of choice for what is judged to be their own good.

30. **"Prospect Theory":** the title of a seminal paper in behavioral economics, published by Daniel Kahneman and Amos Tversky in *Econometrica* in 1979.

31. **Randomized controlled trial (RCT):** the gold-standard methodology used in the social sciences to evaluate the effectiveness of an intervention.

32. **Rational actor:** a person who behaves according to the assumptions of rational choice theory.

33. **Rational choice theory:** the main framework used in neoclassical economics for understanding human behavior in social and economic contexts.

34. **"Regulation for Conservatives":** the title of a 2003 paper by the behavioral economist Colin Camerer and colleagues. It introduced the philosophy of "asymmetric paternalism," which is very similar to *Nudge*'s "libertarian paternalism."

35. **Republican party:** one of the two main political parties in the United States. Founded in 1854, it is associated with right-wing politics.

36. *Science:* one of the world's most prestigious scientific journals, in publication since 1880.

37. **Social and Behavioral Sciences Team:** a group formally established by executive order of President Barack Obama in 2015 to promote the use of behavioral science in the US government.

38. *The Theory of Moral Sentiments:* a book by the Scottish philosopher Adam Smith published in 1759, considered to be the foundational text of the field of behavioral economics.

39. **Third way:** a term for a political position, used by many different politicians during the twentieth century, that attempts to reconcile differences in right- and left-wing political ideology by adopting policies from both points of

view. Thaler and Sunstein argue that the policy ideas in *Nudge* represent a "real third way."

40. **2008 financial crisis:** a period of economic recession considered to be the worst in the developed world since the Great Depression of the 1930s.

41. **World Bank:** an international organization designed to reduce global poverty by providing loans to developing countries for infrastructural development.

42. **World War II:** the global conflict that took place between 1939 and 1945 between Germany, Italy, and Japan (the Axis powers) and Britain, the Soviet Union, the United States, and other nations (the Allies). One of the defining events of the twentieth century.

1. **John Beshears** is a professor of business administration at Harvard Business School. His research applies behavioral economics to individual decision-making and market outcomes.

2. **Luc Bovens (b. 1961)** is a Belgian professor of philosophy at the London School of Economics who has written on the ethics of nudging.

3. **Colin Camerer (b. 1959)** is an American behavioral economist and professor of behavioral finance and economics at the California Institute of Technology. He is part of a group of academics who developed the concept of "asymmetric paternalism," a similar philosophy to "libertarian paternalism."

4. **David Cameron (b. 1966)** is the current prime minister of the United Kingdom, in office since 2010.

5. **Werner De Bondt** is a Belgian economist who has collaborated with Richard H. Thaler in the field of behavioral finance.

6. **Milton Friedman (1912–2006)** was the winner of the Nobel Prize in Economics in 1976 and one of the most influential economists of the twentieth century. He is strongly associated with the Chicago school of economic thought.

7. **David Halpern** is a British psychologist, director of the Behavioural Insights Team, also known as the Nudge Unit.

8. **Christine Jolls (b. 1967)** is an American law professor at Yale Law School who has written on the applications of behavioral economics to matters of law.

9. **Daniel Kahneman (b. 1934)** is an Israeli psychologist, winner of the Nobel Prize in Economics in 2002 for his work on decision-making with Amos Tversky, and professor emeritus of psychology and public affairs at Princeton University.

10. **David Laibson (b. 1966)** is an American behavioral economist and professor of economics at Harvard University. He has written several influential papers applying the idea of limited self-control to economic behavior.

11. **George Loewenstein (b. 1955)** is an American behavioral economist and

professor of economics and psychology at Carnegie Mellon University. He coauthored with Colin Camerer an influential text describing the history of behavioral economics.

12. **Pete Lunn** is an Irish economist who has written on the applications of behavioral economics to matters of regulation and public policy.

13. **Brigitte Madrian** is an American professor of public policy at the Harvard Kennedy School of Harvard University. In 2000 she wrote an influential article with Dennis Shea that demonstrated the importance of default rules in pension-enrollment programs.

14. **Susan Michie (b. 1955)** is a British professor of health psychology at University College London. She has criticized the limits of nudging for health interventions and developed an alternative framework called the Behaviour Change Wheel.

15. **Ed Miliband (b. 1969)** is a British politician and former leader of the Labour party between 2010 and 2015.

16. **Baroness Julia Neuberger (b. 1950)** is a member of the House of Lords (the upper chamber of the British Parliament). She headed that institution's 2011 report on behavior change, which examined the efficacy of nudging.

17. **Barack Obama (b. 1961)** is the 44th president of the United States, elected in 2009 and scheduled to serve until 2017.

18. **George Osborne (b. 1971)** is first secretary of state and chancellor of the exchequer of the United Kingdom.

19. **Richard Posner (b. 1939)** is an American legal scholar, economist, and noted critic of behavioral economics.

20. **Barry Schwartz (b. 1946)** is an American psychologist who has written on the psychology of human decision-making.

21. **Dennis Shea** was the vice-president of American health care company United Health Group in 2000. He conducted a study on pension auto-enrollment with Brigitte Madrian.

22. **Herbert Simon (1916–2001)** was an American academic and winner of the

Nobel Prize in Economics in 1978. He introduced the concept of "bounded rationality" as a basis for understanding human decision-making.

23. **Adam Smith (1723–90)** was a Scottish philosopher who is considered a founding figure of the fields of economics and behavioral economics for his books *The Wealth of Nations* and *The Theory of Moral Sentiments*.

24. **Amos Tversky (1937–96)** was an Israeli psychologist known for his work with Daniel Kahneman on human decision-making.

WORKS CITED

1. Anderson, Joel. "Review of *Nudge: Improving Decisions and Health, Wealth, and Happiness*." *Economics and Philosophy* 26, no. 3 (2010): 369–76.

2. Becker, Gary. "Irrational Behavior and Economic Theory." *Journal of Political Economy* 70, no. 1 (1962): 1–13.

3. "Behavioural Finance to the Rescue?" *Economist*, August 18, 2009. Accessed September 26, 2015. http://www.economist.com/blogs/freeexchange/2009/08/behavioural_finance_to_the_res.

4. Behavioural Insights Team. "Applying Behavioural Insights to Charitable Giving." Accessed September 4, 2015. https://www.gov.uk/government/uploads/system/uploads/attachment_data/file/203286/BIT_Charitable_Giving_Paper.pdf.

5. "Applying Behavioural Insights to Reduce Fraud, Error and Debt." February 2012. Accessed September 4, 2015. https://www.gov.uk/government/uploads/system/uploads/attachment_data/file/60539/BIT_FraudErrorDebt_accessible.pdf.

6. "Behavioural Exchange 2014." Accessed September 30, 2015. http://www.behaviouralinsights.co.uk/bx2015/behavioural-exchange-2014/.

7. "The Behavioural Insights Team Update Report 2013–2015." Accessed September 4, 2015. http://www.behaviouralinsights.co.uk/wp-content/uploads/2015/07/BIT_Update-Report-Final-2013–2015.pdf.

8. "Who We Are." Accessed September 4, 2015. http://www.behaviouralinsights.co.uk/about-us/.

9. Bennhold, Katrin. "Britain's Ministry of Nudges." *New York Times*, December 7, 2013. Accessed September 4, 2015. http://www.nytimes.com/2013/12/08/business/international/britains-ministry-of-nudges.html?_r=0.

10. Beshears, John, James J. Choi, David Laibson, and Brigitte C. Madrian. "How Are Preferences Revealed?" *Journal of Public Economics* 92 (2008): 1787–94.

11. "Best Business Books." *Financial Times*, 2008. Accessed September 4, 2015. http://ig.ft.com/sites/business-book-award/books/2008/longlist/nudge-by-richard-thaler-and-cass-sunstein.

12. Bovens, Luc. "The Ethics of Nudge." In *Preference Change: Approaches from Philosophy, Economics and Psychology*, edited by Till Grüne-Yanoff and Sven Ove Hansson, 207–19. New York: Springer, 2009.

13. Camerer, Colin, and George Loewenstein. "Behavioral Economics: Past, Present, Future." In *Advances in Behavioral Economics*, edited by Colin Camerer, George

Loewenstein, and Matthew Rabin. Princeton, NJ: Princeton University Press, 2003.

14. Camerer, Colin, Samuel Issacharoff, George Loewenstein, Ted O'Donoghue, and Matthew Rabin. "Regulation for Conservatives: Behavioral Economics and the Case for 'Asymmetric Paternalism.'" *University of Pennsylvania Law Review* 151, no. 3 (2003): 1211–54.

15. Cameron, David. "The Next Age of Government." *TED*, February 2010. Accessed September 4, 2015. http://www.ted.com/talks/david_cameron?language=en.

16. Cassidy, John. "After the Blowup." *New Yorker*, January 11, 2010. Accessed September 26, 2015. http://www.newyorker.com/magazine/2010/01/11/after-the-blowup.

17. Clement, Douglas. "Interview with Richard H. Thaler." *The Region Magazine*, October 3, 2013. Accessed September 4, 2015. https://www.minneapolisfed. org/publications/the-region/interview-with-richard-thaler.

18. Day, Elizabeth. "Julia Neuberger: 'A Nudge in the Right Direction Won't Run the Big Society.'" *Observer*, July 17, 2011. Accessed September 4, 2015. http://www.theguardian.com/society/2011/jul/17/julia-neuberger-nudge-big-society.

19. De Bondt, Werner, and Richard H. Thaler. "Does the Stock Market Overreact?" *Journal of Finance* 40, no. 3 (1985): 793–805.

20. Erta, Kristine, Stefan Hunt, Zanna Iscenko, and Will Brambley. "Applying Behavioural Economics at the Financial Conduct Authority." *FCA Occasional Paper* no. 1 (2013). Accessed September 4, 2015. https://www.fca.org.uk/static/documents/occasional-papers/occasional-paper-1.pdf.

21. "Executive Summary of Financial Regulatory Reform: A New Foundation." US Treasury Department, June 17, 2009. Accessed September 4, 2015. http://www.treasury.gov/initiatives/wsr/Documents/executive_summary.pdf.

22. Friedman, Benjamin M. "Guiding Forces." *New York Times*, August 22, 2008. Accessed September 5, 2015. http://www.nytimes.com/2008/08/24/books/review/Friedman-t.html?pagewanted=all&_r=0.

23. FT View, "Economics Needs to Reflect a Post-Crisis World." *Financial Times*, September 25, 2014. Accessed October 15, 2015. http://www.ft.com/cms/s/0/f9f65e88-44a3-11e4-ab0c-00144feabdc0.html#axzz3ojq0z1zz.

24. Goldstein, Daniel G., Eric J. Johnson, Andreas Herrmann, and Mark Heitmann. "Nudge Your Customers toward Better Choices." *Harvard Business Review*, December 2008. Accessed September 4, 2015. https://hbr.org/2008/12/nudge-your-customers-toward-better-choices.

25. Goodwin, Neva, Jonathan Harris, Julie A. Nelson, Brian Roach, and Mariano Torras. *Microeconomics in Context.* 3rd edn. Abingdon: Routledge, 2013.

26. *Google Scholar.* List of texts that have cited *Nudge* as of September 26, 2015. Accessed October 15, 2015. https://scholar.google.com/scholar?cites=168544684 77297806637&as_sdt=2005&sciodt=0,5&hl=en.

27. Halonen, Elina. "Research Heroes: Richard H. Thaler." *InDecision Blog*, January 15, 2013. Accessed September 4, 2015. http://indecisionblog.com/2013/01/15/ research-heroes-richard-thaler/.

28. Haynes, Laura, Owain Service, Ben Goldacre, and David Torgerson. "Test, Learn, Adapt: Developing Public Policy with Randomised Controlled Trials." Cabinet Office, 2012. Accessed September 4, 2015. https://www.gov.uk/ government/ uploads/system/uploads/attachment_data/file/62529/TLA-1906126. pdf.

29. House of Lords Science and Technology Select Committee. "Behaviour Change Report." *HL Paper* 179 (2011). Accessed September 4, 2015. http://www. publications.parliament.uk/pa/ld201012/ldselect/ldsctech/179/179.pdf.

30. Housel, Morgan. "Daniel Kahneman on Challenging Economic Assumptions." *Motley Fool*, June 29, 2013. Accessed September 4, 2015. http://www.fool. com/ investing/general/2013/06/29/challenging-assumptions-an-economist-considers-psy.aspx.

31. Jolls, Christine, Cass R. Sunstein, and Richard H. Thaler. "A Behavioral Approach to Law and Economics." *Stanford Law Review* 50, no. 5 (1998): 1471–550.

32. Kahneman, Daniel. *Thinking, Fast and Slow.* New York: Farrar, Straus and Giroux, 2011.

33. Kahneman, Daniel, and Amos Tversky. "Prospect Theory: An Analysis of Decision under Risk." *Econometrica* 47, no. 2 (1979): 263–92.

34. Kalil, Tom. "Funding What Works: The Importance of Low-Cost Randomized Controlled Trials." *White House Blog*, July 9, 2014. Accessed September 4, 2015. https://www.whitehouse.gov/blog/2014/07/09/funding-what-works-importance-low-cost-randomized-controlled-trials.

35. Karp, Gregory. "Profile: Richard H. Thaler, University of Chicago Booth School of Business Professor." *Chicago Tribune*, April 30, 2012. Accessed September 4, 2015. http://articles.chicagotribune.com/2012-04-30/business/ct-biz-0430–executive-profile-thaler-20120430_1_economics-daniel-kahneman-cost-fallacy.

36. Krugman, Paul. "How Did Economists Get It So Wrong?" *New York Times,*

September 6, 2009. Accessed September 26, 2015. http://www.econ.ucdavis. edu/faculty/kdsalyer/LECTURES/Ecn200e/krugman_macro.pdf.

37. Kuang, Cliff. "In the Cafeteria, Google Gets Healthy." *Fast Company Magazine*, March 19, 2012. Accessed September 4, 2015. http://www.fastcompany. com/1822516/cafeteria-google-gets-healthy.

38. Laibson, David. "Golden Eggs and Hyperbolic Discounting." *Quarterly Journal of Economics* 112 no. 2 (1997): 443–78.

39. Leonard, Thomas C. "Richard H. Thaler, Cass R. Sunstein, 'Nudge: Improving Decisions about Health, Wealth, and Happiness.'" *Constitutional Political Economy Book Review*, 2008. Accessed September 4, 2015. http://www. princeton.edu/~tleonard/reviews/nudge.pdf.

40. Lunn, Pete. *Regulatory Policy and Behavioural Economics*. Paris: OECD Publishing, 2014.

41. Madrian, Brigitte, and Dennis Shea. "The Power of Suggestion: Inertia in 401(k) Participation and Savings Behavior." *Quarterly Journal of Economics* 116, no. 4 (2001): 1149–87.

42. Marteau, Theresa M., David Ogilvie, Martin Roland, Marc Suhrcke, and Michael P. Kelly. "Judging Nudging: Can Nudging Improve Population Health?" *British Medical Journal* 342 (2011).

43. Michie, Susan, Maartje M. van Stralen, and Robert West. "The Behaviour Change Wheel: A New Method for Characterising and Designing Behaviour Change Interventions." *Implementation Science* 6, no. 42 (2011).

44. Nickerson, David W., and Todd Rogers. "Do You Have a Voting Plan? Implementation Intentions, Voter Turnout, and Organic Plan Making." *Psychological Science* 21, no. 2 (2010): 194–9.

45. Orwid, John. "Behavioral Economics Gives the Advertising Industry a Nudge in the Right Direction." *Forbes*, February 5, 2014. Accessed September 26, 2015. http://www.forbes.com/sites/johnowrid/2014/02/05/behavioural-economics-gives-the-advertising-industry-a-nudge-in-the-right-direction/.

46. Osborne, George. "Nudge, Nudge, Win, Win." *Guardian*, July 14, 2008. Accessed September 4, 2015. http://www.theguardian.com/commentisfree/2008/jul/14/conservatives.economy.

47. "Pick of the Pile." *Economist*, December 4, 2008. Accessed September 4, 2015. http://www.economist.com/node/12719711.

48. Posner, Richard A. "Treating Financial Consumers as Consenting Adults." *Wall

Street Journal, July 22, 2009. Accessed September 4, 2015. http://www.wsj.com/articles/SB10001424052970203946904574302213213148166.

49. Schnellenbach, Jan, and Christian Schubert. "Behavioral Political Economy: A Survey." *European Journal of Political Economy*, in press (2015).

50. Schwartz, Barry. "Why Not Nudge? A Review of Cass R. Sunstein's *Why Nudge?*" *thepsychreport*, April 17, 2014. Accessed September 4, 2015. http://thepsychreport.com/essays-discussion/nudge-review-cass-sunsteins-why-nudge/.

51. Shafir, Eldar (ed.). *The Behavioral Foundations of Public Policy*. Princeton, NJ: Princeton University Press, 2012.

52. Smith, Noah. "Five Economists Who Deserve Nobels." *Bloomberg View*, December 9, 2014. Accessed September 4, 2015. http://www.bloombergview.com/articles/2014-12-09/five-economists-who-deserve-nobels.

53. Social and Behavioral Sciences Team. "Social and Behavioral Sciences Team Annual Report." Executive Office of the President National Science and Technology Council, September 2015. Accessed September 30, 2015. https://www.whitehouse.gov/sites/default/files/microsites/ostp/sbst_2015_annual_report_final_9_14_15.pdf.

54. Sparrow, Andrew. "Fabian Conference—Live." *Guardian*, January 17, 2009. Accessed September 4, 2015. http://www.theguardian.com/politics/blog/2009/jan/17/fabian-conference-blog.

55. Sunstein, Cass R. "The Council of Psychological Advisers." *Annual Review of Psychology*. Accessed September 4, 2015. http://dash.harvard.edu/bitstream/handle/1/13031653/annualreview9_15.pdf?sequence=1.

56. "Nudges: Good and Bad." *New York Review of Books*, October 23, 2014. Accessed September 4, 2015. http://www.nybooks.com/articles/archives/2014/oct/23/nudges-good-and-bad/.

57. *Simpler: The Future of Government*. New York: Simon & Schuster, 2013.

58. "There's a Backlash against Nudging—But It Was Never Meant to Solve Every Problem." *Guardian*, April 24, 2014. Accessed September 4, 2015. http://www.theguardian.com/commentisfree/2014/apr/24/nudge-backlash-free-society-dignity-coercion.

59. *Why Nudge?* New York: Yale University Press, 2014.

60. "Sveriges Riksbank Prize in Economic Sciences in Memory of Alfred Nobel, 2002." *Nobelprize.org*. Accessed September 4, 2015. http://www.nobelprize.org/nobel_prizes/economic-sciences/laureates/2002/.

61. Thaler, Richard H. "Anomalies." Accessed September 4, 2015. http://faculty. chicagobooth.edu/Richard.Thaler/research/anomalies.html.

62. "Do You Need a Nudge?" *Yale Insights*, November 4, 2009. Accessed September 4, 2015. http://insights.som.yale.edu/insights/do-you-need-nudge.

63. "Thaler Responds to Posner on Consumer Protection." *PBS Newshour*, July 28, 2009. Accessed September 4, 2015. http://www.pbs.org/newshour/making-sense/thaler-responds-to-posner-on-c/.

64. "Watching Behavior before Writing the Rules." *New York Times*, July 7, 2012. Accessed September 4, 2015. http://www.nytimes.com/2012/07/08/business/ behavioral-science-can-help-guide-policy-economic-view.html.

65. "When Will There Be a Single Unified 'Behavioral' Theory of Economic Activity?" in "What's the Question about Your Field That You Dread Being Asked?" *Edge*, March 28, 2013. Accessed September 4, 2015. http://edge. org/conversation/whats-the-question-about-your-field-that-you-dread-being-asked#25056.

66. Thaler, Richard H., and Cass R. Sunstein. "Libertarian Paternalism Is Not an Oxymoron." *University of Chicago Law Review* 70, no. 4 (2003): 1159–1202.

67. "Libertarian Paternalism." *The American Economic Review* 93, no. 2 (2003): 175–9.

68. *Nudge: Improving Decisions about Health, Wealth, and Happiness*. New York: Yale University Press, 2008.

69. Tversky, Amos, and Daniel Kahneman. "Judgment under Uncertainty: Heuristics and Biases." *Science* 185, no. 4157 (1974): 1124–31.

70. Ubel, Peter. "Q & A with Richard H. Thaler on What It Really Means to Be a 'Nudge.'" *Forbes*, February 20, 2015. Accessed September 4, 2015. http://www. forbes.com/sites/peterubel/2015/02/20/q-a-with-richard-thaler-on-what-it-really-means-to-be-a-nudge/.

71. Varian, Hal. *Intermediate Microeconomics*. 8th edn. New York: W. W. Norton & Company, 2009.

72. Waldron, Jeremy. "It's All for Your Own Good." *New York Review of Books*, October 9, 2014. Accessed September 4, 2015. http://www.nybooks.com/ articles/archives/2014/oct/09/cass-sunstein-its-all-your-own-good/.

73. White House. "Executive Order—Using Behavioral Science Insights to Better Serve the American People." Office of the Press Secretary, September 15, 2015. Accessed September 30, 2015. https://www.whitehouse.gov/the-press-

office/2015/09/15/executive-order-using-behavioral-science-insights-better-serve-american.

74. Wolfers, Justin. "A Better Government, One Tweak at a Time." *New York Times*, September 25, 2015. Accessed September 30, 2015. http://www.nytimes.com/2015/09/27/upshot/a-better-government-one-tweak-at-a-time.html?rref=upshot&_r=0.

75. World Bank. "Mind, Society, and Behavior," *World Bank Group Flagship Report*, 2015. Accessed September 26, 2015. www.worldbank.org/content/dam/Worldbank/Publications/WDR/WDR%202015/WDR-2015-Full-Report.pdf.

76. Zipkin, Nina. "Attention, Apple Shoppers: You're Being Followed." December 6, 2013. Accessed September 4, 2015. http://www.entrepreneur.com/ article/230275.

原书作者简介

理查德·H.泰勒生于 1945 年，被誉为"行为经济学之父"，被认为是未来诺贝尔经济学奖的有力竞争者（泰勒于 2017 年获得诺贝尔经济学奖——译者加）。卡斯·R.桑斯坦生于 1954 年，于 2009 年至 2012 年任贝拉克·奥巴马政府信息与法规事务办公室主任，是目前全球被引用最多的法学家之一。泰勒和桑斯坦同在芝加哥大学执教，两人合著了《助推》，提出政府能够在尊重民众自由选择权的同时帮助他们做出更明智的决策。该书被《经济学人》杂志评为"2008 年度最佳图书"之一。

本书作者简介

马克·伊根是英国斯特林大学管理学院行为科学专业的博士生，曾在荷兰马斯特里赫特大学学习人类决策科学，并获得理学硕士学位。他是英国行为洞察团队成员之一，为英国政府提供决策咨询。

世界名著中的批判性思维

《世界思想宝库钥匙丛书》致力于深入浅出地阐释全世界著名思想家的观点，不论是谁、在何处都能了解到，从而推进批判性思维发展。

《世界思想宝库钥匙丛书》与世界顶尖大学的一流学者合作，为一系列学科中最有影响的著作推出新的分析文本，介绍其观点和影响。在这一不断扩展的系列中，每种选入的著作都代表了历经时间考验的思想典范。通过为这些著作提供必要背景、揭示原作者的学术渊源以及说明这些著作所产生的影响，本系列图书希望让读者以新视角看待这些划时代的经典之作。读者应学会思考、运用并挑战这些著作中的观点，而不是简单接受它们。

ABOUT THE AUTHOR OF THE ORIGINAL WORK

US economist **Richard H. Thaler** (b. 1945) is credited with being a founding father of the field of behavioral economics and has been tipped as a future Nobel Prize winner. His colleague, the legal scholar **Cass R. Sunstein** (b. 1954), served in the administration of Barack Obama from 2009 to 2012 and is one of the most frequently cited legal scholars in the world today. Both men taught at the University of Chicago and collaborated on their influential 2008 book *Nudge: Improving Decisions about Health, Wealth, and Happiness*, which argued that governments can help people make better decisions, while still respecting their freedom of choice. It was named one of the best books of 2008 by respected magazine *The Economist*.

ABOUT THE AUTHORS OF THE ANALYSIS

Mark Egan is a doctoral candidate in behavioural science at the University of Stirling Management School. He holds an MSc in human decision science from Maastricht University and, in addition to his doctoral research, works with the Behavioural Insights Team advising the UK government on behavioural science and policy decisions.

ABOUT MACAT
GREAT WORKS FOR CRITICAL THINKING

Macat is focused on making the ideas of the world's great thinkers accessible and comprehensible to everybody, everywhere, in ways that promote the development of enhanced critical thinking skills.

It works with leading academics from the world's top universities to produce new analyses that focus on the ideas and the impact of the most influential works ever written across a wide variety of academic disciplines. Each of the works that sit at the heart of its growing library is an enduring example of great thinking. But by setting them in context—and looking at the influences that shaped their authors, as well as the responses they provoked—Macat encourages readers to look at these classics and game-changers with fresh eyes. Readers learn to think, engage and challenge their ideas, rather than simply accepting them.

批判性思维与《助推》

首要批判性思维技能：理性化思维

次要批判性思维技能：创造性思维

理查德·H.泰勒和卡斯·R.桑斯坦的著作《助推：如何做出有关健康、财富和幸福的更优决策》于2008年出版，很快就成为现代经济学和政治学领域中最具影响力的书籍之一，并在短时间内，影响了美国、英国以及新加坡等国政府部门的公共决策。

泰勒和桑斯坦的这一力作大获成功，主要原因之一在于该书用令人信服的论据详细阐明了他们提出的经济决策理念。《助推》不是一本充满原始发现或数据的书，相反，它谨慎、系统地综合分析了行为经济学数十年以来的研究成果。总体而言，传统经济学研究以人类理性决策假设为基础。而《助推》挑战了传统经济学理论基础，它关注影响人类决策的"非理性"认知偏差，而这些认知偏差说明了某些类型的经济决策是可预测的非理性行为。

泰勒和桑斯坦具有非凡的论证能力，有效地反驳了各种反对助推的观点。他们认为，如果政府能充分理解这些认知偏差，就可以"助推"民众做出更明智的选择。《助推》是一部充满智慧、饶有趣味、运用各种说理技巧、极具信服力的著作。

CRITICAL THINKING AND *NUDGE*

- Primary critical thinking skill: REASONING
- Secondary critical thinking skill: CREATIVE THINKING

When it was published in 2008, Richard H. Thaler and Cass R. Sunstein's *Nudge: Improving Decisions about Health, Wealth, and Happiness* quickly became one of the most influential books in modern economics and politics. Within a short time, it had inspired whole government departments in the US and UK, and others as far afield as Singapore.

One of the keys to *Nudge*'s success is Thaler and Sunstein's ability to create a detailed and persuasive case for their take on economic decision-making. *Nudge* is not a book packed with original findings or data; instead it is a careful and systematic synthesis of decades of research into behavioral economics. The discipline challenges much conventional economic thought—which works on the basis that, overall, humans make rational decisions—by focusing instead on the "irrational" cognitive biases that affect our decision making.These seemingly in-built biases mean that certain kinds of economic decision-making are predictably irrational.

Thaler and Sunstein prove themselves experts at creating persuasive arguments and dealing effectively with counter-arguments.They conclude that if governments understand these cognitive biases, they can "nudge" us into making better decisions for ourselves. Entertaining as well as smart, Nudge shows the full range of reasoning skills that go into making a persuasive argument.

《世界思想宝库钥匙丛书》简介

《世界思想宝库钥匙丛书》致力于为一系列在各领域产生重大影响的人文社科类经典著作提供独特的学术探讨。每一本读物都不仅仅是原经典著作的内容摘要，而是介绍并深入研究原经典著作的学术渊源、主要观点和历史影响。这一丛书的目的是提供一套学习资料，以促进读者掌握批判性思维，从而更全面、深刻地去理解重要思想。

每一本读物分为 3 个部分：学术渊源、学术思想和学术影响，每个部分下有 4 个小节。这些章节旨在从各个方面研究原经典著作及其反响。

由于独特的体例，每一本读物不但易于阅读，而且另有一项优点：所有读物的编排体例相同，读者在进行某个知识层面的调查或研究时可交叉参阅多本该丛书中的相关读物，从而开启跨领域研究的路径。

为了方便阅读，每本读物最后还列出了术语表和人名表（在书中则以星号 * 标记），此外还有参考文献。

《世界思想宝库钥匙丛书》与剑桥大学合作，理清了批判性思维的要点，即如何通过 6 种技能来进行有效思考。其中 3 种技能让我们能够理解问题，另 3 种技能让我们有能力解决问题。这 6 种技能合称为"批判性思维 PACIER 模式"，它们是：

分析：了解如何建立一个观点；

评估：研究一个观点的优点和缺点；

阐释：对意义所产生的问题加以理解；

创造性思维：提出新的见解，发现新的联系；

解决问题：提出切实有效的解决办法；

理性化思维：创建有说服力的观点。

THE MACAT LIBRARY

The Macat Library is a series of unique academic explorations of seminal works in the humanities and social sciences — books and papers that have had a significant and widely recognised impact on their disciplines. It has been created to serve as much more than just a summary of what lies between the covers of a great book. It illuminates and explores the influences on, ideas of, and impact of that book. Our goal is to offer a learning resource that encourages critical thinking and fosters a better, deeper understanding of important ideas.

Each publication is divided into three Sections: Influences, Ideas, and Impact. Each Section has four Modules. These explore every important facet of the work, and the responses to it.

This Section-Module structure makes a Macat Library book easy to use, but it has another important feature. Because each Macat book is written to the same format, it is possible (and encouraged!) to cross-reference multiple Macat books along the same lines of inquiry or research. This allows the reader to open up interesting interdisciplinary pathways.

To further aid your reading, lists of glossary terms and people mentioned are included at the end of this book (these are indicated by an asterisk [*] throughout) — as well as a list of works cited.

Macat has worked with the University of Cambridge to identify the elements of critical thinking and understand the ways in which six different skills combine to enable effective thinking.

Three allow us to fully understand a problem; three more give us the tools to solve it. Together, these six skills make up the PACIER model of critical thinking. They are:

ANALYSIS — understanding how an argument is built
EVALUATION — exploring the strengths and weaknesses of an argument
INTERPRETATION — understanding issues of meaning
CREATIVE THINKING — coming up with new ideas and fresh connections
PROBLEM-SOLVING — producing strong solutions
REASONING — creating strong arguments

"《世界思想宝库钥匙丛书》提供了独一无二的跨学科学习和研究工具。它介绍那些革新了各自学科研究的经典著作，还邀请全世界一流专家和教育机构进行严谨的分析，为每位读者打开世界顶级教育的大门。"

—— 安德烈亚斯·施莱歇尔，
经济合作与发展组织教育与技能司司长

"《世界思想宝库钥匙丛书》直面大学教育的巨大挑战……他们组建了一支精干而活跃的学者队伍，来推出在研究广度上颇具新意的教学材料。"

—— 布罗尔斯教授、勋爵，剑桥大学前校长

"《世界思想宝库钥匙丛书》的愿景令人赞叹。它通过分析和阐释那些曾深刻影响人类思想以及社会、经济发展的经典文本，提供了新的学习方法。它推动批判性思维，这对于任何社会和经济体来说都是至关重要的。这就是未来的学习方法。"

—— 查尔斯·克拉克阁下，英国前教育大臣

"对于那些影响了各自领域的著作，《世界思想宝库钥匙丛书》能让人们立即了解到围绕那些著作展开的评论性言论，这让该系列图书成为在这些领域从事研究的师生们不可或缺的资源。"

—— 威廉·特朗佐教授，加利福尼亚大学圣地亚哥分校

"Macat offers an amazing first-of-its-kind tool for interdisciplinary learning and research. Its focus on works that transformed their disciplines and its rigorous approach, drawing on the world's leading experts and educational institutions, opens up a world-class education to anyone."

—— Andreas Schleicher, Director for Education and Skills, Organisation for Economic Co-operation and Development

"Macat is taking on some of the major challenges in university education... They have drawn together a strong team of active academics who are producing teaching materials that are novel in the breadth of their approach."

—— Prof Lord Broers, former Vice-Chancellor of the University of Cambridge

"The Macat vision is exceptionally exciting. It focuses upon new modes of learning which analyse and explain seminal texts which have profoundly influenced world thinking and so social and economic development. It promotes the kind of critical thinking which is essential for any society and economy. This is the learning of the future."

—— Rt Hon Charles Clarke, former UK Secretary of State for Education

"The Macat analyses provide immediate access to the critical conversation surrounding the books that have shaped their respective discipline, which will make them an invaluable resource to all of those, students and teachers, working in the field."

—— Prof William Tronzo, University of California at San Diego

TITLE	中文书名	类别
An Analysis of Arjun Appadurai's *Modernity at Large: Cultural Dimensions of Globalisation*	解析阿尔君·阿帕杜莱《消失的现代性：全球化的文化维度》	人类学
An Analysis of Claude Lévi-Strauss's *Structural Anthropology*	解析克劳德·列维-斯特劳斯《结构人类学》	人类学
An Analysis of Marcel Mauss's *The Gift*	解析马塞尔·莫斯《礼物》	人类学
An Analysis of Jared M. Diamond's *Guns, Germs, and Steel: The Fate of Human Societies*	解析贾雷德·戴蒙德《枪炮、病菌与钢铁：人类社会的命运》	人类学
An Analysis of Clifford Geertz's *The Interpretation of Cultures*	解析克利福德·格尔茨《文化的解释》	人类学
An Analysis of Philippe Ariès's *Centuries of Childhood: A Social History of Family Life*	解析菲力浦·阿利埃斯《儿童的世纪：旧制度下的儿童和家庭生活》	人类学
An Analysis of W. Chan Kim & Renée Mauborgne's *Blue Ocean Strategy*	解析金伟灿/勒妮·莫博涅《蓝海战略》	商业
An Analysis of John P. Kotter's *Leading Change*	解析约翰·P.科特《领导变革》	商业
An Analysis of Michael E. Porter's *Competitive Strategy: Techniques for Analyzing Industries and Competitors*	解析迈克尔·E.波特《竞争战略：分析产业和竞争对手的技术》	商业
An Analysis of Jean Lave & Etienne Wenger's *Situated Learning: Legitimate Peripheral Participation*	解析琼·莱夫/艾蒂纳·温格《情境学习：合法的边缘性参与》	商业
An Analysis of Douglas McGregor's *The Human Side of Enterprise*	解析道格拉斯·麦格雷戈《企业的人性面》	商业
An Analysis of Milton Friedman's *Capitalism and Freedom*	解析米尔顿·弗里德曼《资本主义与自由》	商业
An Analysis of Ludwig von Mises's *The Theory of Money and Credit*	解析路德维希·冯·米塞斯《货币和信用理论》	经济学
An Analysis of Adam Smith's *The Wealth of Nations*	解析亚当·斯密《国富论》	经济学
An Analysis of Thomas Piketty's *Capital in the Twenty-First Century*	解析托马斯·皮凯蒂《21世纪资本论》	经济学
An Analysis of Nassim Nicholas Taleb's *The Black Swan: The Impact of the Highly Improbable*	解析纳西姆·尼古拉斯·塔勒布《黑天鹅：如何应对不可预知的未来》	经济学
An Analysis of Ha-Joon Chang's *Kicking Away the Ladder*	解析张夏准《富国陷阱：发达国家为何踢开梯子》	经济学
An Analysis of Thomas Robert Malthus's *An Essay on the Principle of Population*	解析托马斯·马尔萨斯《人口论》	经济学

An Analysis of John Maynard Keynes's *The General Theory of Employment, Interest and Money*	解析约翰·梅纳德·凯恩斯《就业、利息和货币通论》	经济学
An Analysis of Milton Friedman's *The Role of Monetary Policy*	解析米尔顿·弗里德曼《货币政策的作用》	经济学
An Analysis of Burton G. Malkiel's *A Random Walk Down Wall Street*	解析伯顿·G.马尔基尔《漫步华尔街》	经济学
An Analysis of Friedrich A. Hayek's *The Road to Serfdom*	解析弗里德里希·A.哈耶克《通往奴役之路》	经济学
An Analysis of Charles P. Kindleberger's *Manias, Panics, and Crashes: A History of Financial Crises*	解析查尔斯·P.金德尔伯格《疯狂、惊恐和崩溃：金融危机史》	经济学
An Analysis of Amartya Sen's *Development as Freedom*	解析阿马蒂亚·森《以自由看待发展》	经济学
An Analysis of Rachel Carson's *Silent Spring*	解析蕾切尔·卡森《寂静的春天》	地理学
An Analysis of Charles Darwin's *On the Origin of Species: by Means of Natural Selection, or The Preservation of Favoured Races in the Struggle for Life*	解析查尔斯·达尔文《物种起源》	地理学
An Analysis of World Commission on Environment and Development's *The Brundtland Report, Our Common Future*	解析世界环境与发展委员会《布伦特兰报告：我们共同的未来》	地理学
An Analysis of James E. Lovelock's *Gaia: A New Look at Life on Earth*	解析詹姆斯·E.拉伍洛克《盖娅：地球生命的新视野》	地理学
An Analysis of Paul Kennedy's *The Rise and Fall of the Great Powers: Economic Change and Military Conflict from 1500—2000*	解析保罗·肯尼迪《大国的兴衰：1500—2000年的经济变革与军事冲突》	历史
An Analysis of Janet L. Abu-Lughod's *Before European Hegemony: The World System A. D. 1250—1350*	解析珍妮特·L.阿布-卢格霍德《欧洲霸权之前：1250—1350年的世界体系》	历史
An Analysis of Alfred W. Crosby's *The Columbian Exchange: Biological and Cultural Consequences of 1492*	解析艾尔弗雷德·W.克罗斯比《哥伦布大交换：1492年以后的生物影响和文化冲击》	历史
An Analysis of Tony Judt's *Postwar: A History of Europe since 1945*	解析托尼·朱特《战后欧洲史》	历史
An Analysis of Richard J. Evans's *In Defence of History*	解析理查德·J.艾文斯《捍卫历史》	历史
An Analysis of Eric Hobsbawm's *The Age of Revolution: Europe 1789–1848*	解析艾瑞克·霍布斯鲍姆《革命的年代：欧洲1789—1848年》	历史

An Analysis of Roland Barthes's *Mythologies*	解析罗兰·巴特《神话学》	文学与批判理论
An Analysis of Simon de Beauvoir's *The Second Sex*	解析西蒙娜·德·波伏娃《第二性》	文学与批判理论
An Analysis of Edward W. Said's *Orientalism*	解析爱德华·W. 萨义德《东方主义》	文学与批判理论
An Analysis of Virginia Woolf's *A Room of One's Own*	解析弗吉尼亚·伍尔芙《一间自己的房间》	文学与批判理论
An Analysis of Judith Butler's *Gender Trouble*	解析朱迪斯·巴特勒《性别麻烦》	文学与批判理论
An Analysis of Ferdinand de Saussure's *Course in General Linguistics*	解析费尔迪南·德·索绪尔《普通语言学教程》	文学与批判理论
An Analysis of Susan Sontag's *On Photography*	解析苏珊·桑塔格《论摄影》	文学与批判理论
An Analysis of Walter Benjamin's *The Work of Art in the Age of Mechanical Reproduction*	解析瓦尔特·本雅明《机械复制时代的艺术作品》	文学与批判理论
An Analysis of W.E.B. Du Bois's *The Souls of Black Folk*	解析 W.E.B. 杜波依斯《黑人的灵魂》	文学与批判理论
An Analysis of Plato's *The Republic*	解析柏拉图《理想国》	哲学
An Analysis of Plato's *Symposium*	解析柏拉图《会饮篇》	哲学
An Analysis of Aristotle's *Metaphysics*	解析亚里士多德《形而上学》	哲学
An Analysis of Aristotle's *Nicomachean Ethics*	解析亚里士多德《尼各马可伦理学》	哲学
An Analysis of Immanuel Kant's *Critique of Pure Reason*	解析伊曼努尔·康德《纯粹理性批判》	哲学
An Analysis of Ludwig Wittgenstein's *Philosophical Investigations*	解析路德维希·维特根斯坦《哲学研究》	哲学
An Analysis of G.W.F. Hegel's *Phenomenology of Spirit*	解析 G.W.F. 黑格尔《精神现象学》	哲学
An Analysis of Baruch Spinoza's *Ethics*	解析巴鲁赫·斯宾诺莎《伦理学》	哲学
An Analysis of Hannah Arendt's *The Human Condition*	解析汉娜·阿伦特《人的境况》	哲学
An Analysis of G.E.M. Anscombe's *Modern Moral Philosophy*	解析 G.E.M. 安斯康姆《现代道德哲学》	哲学
An Analysis of David Hume's *An Enquiry Concerning Human Understanding*	解析大卫·休谟《人类理解研究》	哲学

An Analysis of Søren Kierkegaard's *Fear and Trembling*	解析索伦·克尔凯郭尔《恐惧与战栗》	哲学
An Analysis of René Descartes's *Meditations on First Philosophy*	解析勒内·笛卡尔《第一哲学沉思录》	哲学
An Analysis of Friedrich Nietzsche's *On the Genealogy of Morality*	解析弗里德里希·尼采《论道德的谱系》	哲学
An Analysis of Gilbert Ryle's *The Concept of Mind*	解析吉尔伯特·赖尔《心的概念》	哲学
An Analysis of Thomas Kuhn's *The Structure of Scientific Revolutions*	解析托马斯·库恩《科学革命的结构》	哲学
An Analysis of John Stuart Mill's *Utilitarianism*	解析约翰·斯图亚特·穆勒《功利主义》	哲学
An Analysis of Aristotle's *Politics*	解析亚里士多德《政治学》	政治学
An Analysis of Niccolò Machiavelli's *The Prince*	解析尼科洛·马基雅维利《君主论》	政治学
An Analysis of Karl Marx's *Capital*	解析卡尔·马克思《资本论》	政治学
An Analysis of Benedict Anderson's *Imagined Communities*	解析本尼迪克特·安德森《想象的共同体》	政治学
An Analysis of Samuel P. Huntington's *The Clash of Civilizations and the Remaking of World Order*	解析塞缪尔·P.亨廷顿《文明的冲突与世界秩序重建》	政治学
An Analysis of Alexis de Tocqueville's *Democracy in America*	解析阿列克西·德·托克维尔《论美国的民主》	政治学
An Analysis of John A. Hobson's *Imperialism: A Study*	解析约翰·A.霍布森《帝国主义》	政治学
An Analysis of Thomas Paine's *Common Sense*	解析托马斯·潘恩《常识》	政治学
An Analysis of John Rawls's *A Theory of Justice*	解析约翰·罗尔斯《正义论》	政治学
An Analysis of Francis Fukuyama's *The End of History and the Last Man*	解析弗朗西斯·福山《历史的终结与最后的人》	政治学
An Analysis of John Locke's *Two Treatises of Government*	解析约翰·洛克《政府论》	政治学
An Analysis of Sun Tzu's *The Art of War*	解析孙武《孙子兵法》	政治学
An Analysis of Henry Kissinger's *World Order: Reflections on the Character of Nations and the Course of History*	解析亨利·基辛格《世界秩序》	政治学
An Analysis of Jean-Jacques Rousseau's *The Social Contract*	解析让-雅克·卢梭《社会契约论》	政治学

An Analysis of Odd Arne Westad's *The Global Cold War: Third World Interventions and the Making of Our Times*	解析文安立《全球冷战：美苏对第三世界的干涉与当代世界的形成》	政治学
An Analysis of Sigmund Freud's *The Interpretation of Dreams*	解析西格蒙德·弗洛伊德《梦的解析》	心理学
An Analysis of William James' *The Principles of Psychology*	解析威廉·詹姆斯《心理学原理》	心理学
An Analysis of Philip Zimbardo's *The Lucifer Effect*	解析菲利普·津巴多《路西法效应》	心理学
An Analysis of Leon Festinger's *A Theory of Cognitive Dissonance*	解析利昂·费斯汀格《认知失调论》	心理学
An Analysis of Richard H. Thaler & Cass R. Sunstein's *Nudge: Improving Decisions about Health, Wealth, and Happiness*	解析理查德·H. 泰勒 / 卡斯·R. 桑斯坦《助推：如何做出有关健康、财富和幸福的更优决策》	心理学
An Analysis of Gordon Allport's *The Nature of Prejudice*	解析高尔登·奥尔波特《偏见的本质》	心理学
An Analysis of Steven Pinker's *The Better Angels of Our Nature: Why Violence Has Declined*	解析斯蒂芬·平克《人性中的善良天使：暴力为什么会减少》	心理学
An Analysis of Stanley Milgram's *Obedience to Authority*	解析斯坦利·米尔格拉姆《对权威的服从》	心理学
An Analysis of Betty Friedan's *The Feminine Mystique*	解析贝蒂·弗里丹《女性的奥秘》	心理学
An Analysis of David Riesman's *The Lonely Crowd: A Study of the Changing American Character*	解析大卫·理斯曼《孤独的人群：美国人社会性格演变之研究》	社会学
An Analysis of Franz Boas's *Race, Language and Culture*	解析弗朗兹·博厄斯《种族、语言与文化》	社会学
An Analysis of Pierre Bourdieu's *Outline of a Theory of Practice*	解析皮埃尔·布尔迪厄《实践理论大纲》	社会学
An Analysis of Max Weber's *The Protestant Ethic and the Spirit of Capitalism*	解析马克斯·韦伯《新教伦理与资本主义精神》	社会学
An Analysis of Jane Jacobs's *The Death and Life of Great American Cities*	解析简·雅各布斯《美国大城市的死与生》	社会学
An Analysis of C. Wright Mills's *The Sociological Imagination*	解析 C. 赖特·米尔斯《社会学的想象力》	社会学
An Analysis of Robert E. Lucas Jr.'s *Why Doesn't Capital Flow from Rich to Poor Countries?*	解析小罗伯特·E. 卢卡斯《为何资本不从富国流向穷国？》	社会学

An Analysis of Émile Durkheim's *On Suicide*	解析埃米尔·迪尔凯姆《自杀论》	社会学
An Analysis of Eric Hoffer's *The True Believer: Thoughts on the Nature of Mass Movements*	解析埃里克·霍弗《狂热分子：群众运动圣经》	社会学
An Analysis of Jared M. Diamond's *Collapse: How Societies Choose to Fail or Survive*	解析贾雷德·M.戴蒙德《大崩溃：社会如何选择兴亡》	社会学
An Analysis of Michel Foucault's *The History of Sexuality Vol. 1: The Will to Knowledge*	解析米歇尔·福柯《性史（第一卷）：求知意志》	社会学
An Analysis of Michel Foucault's *Discipline and Punish*	解析米歇尔·福柯《规训与惩罚》	社会学
An Analysis of Richard Dawkins's *The Selfish Gene*	解析理查德·道金斯《自私的基因》	社会学
An Analysis of Antonio Gramsci's *Prison Notebooks*	解析安东尼奥·葛兰西《狱中札记》	社会学
An Analysis of Augustine's *Confessions*	解析奥古斯丁《忏悔录》	神学
An Analysis of C.S. Lewis's *The Abolition of Man*	解析C.S.路易斯《人之废》	神学

图书在版编目（CIP）数据

解析理查德·H.泰勒/卡斯·R.桑斯坦《助推：如何做出有关健康、财富和幸福的更优决策》：汉、英 / 马克·伊根（Mark Egan）著．江丹译—上海：上海外语教育出版社，2019（世界思想宝库钥匙丛书）
ISBN 978−7−5446−5923−9

Ⅰ.①解… Ⅱ.①马… ②江… Ⅲ.①决策学—研究—汉、英 Ⅳ.①C934

中国版本图书馆CIP数据核字（2019）第115612号

This Chinese-English bilingual edition of *An Analysis of Richard H. Thaler & Cass R. Sunstein*'s *Nudge: Improving Decisions about Health, Wealth and Happiness* is published by arrangement with Macat International Limited.
Licensed for sale throughout the world.

本书汉英双语版由Macat国际有限公司授权上海外语教育出版社有限公司出版。供在全世界范围内发行、销售。

图字：09−2018−549

出版发行：上海外语教育出版社
　　　　　　（上海外国语大学内）　邮编：200083
电　话：021−65425300（总机）
电子邮箱：bookinfo@sflep.com.cn
网　址：http://www.sflep.com
责任编辑：顾 奕

印　刷：上海华业装璜印刷厂有限公司
开　本：890×1240　1/32　印张 5.625　字数 115千字
版　次：2019 年 10月第 1版　2019 年 10月第 1次印刷
印　数：2 100 册

书　号：ISBN 978-7-5446-5923-9
定　价：30.00 元
　　本版图书如有印装质量问题，可向本社调换
　　质量服务热线：4008-213-263　电子邮箱：**editorial@sflep.com**